Blogging 105

105 Ways to Blog as an Author, an Expert, and a Real Person

John Kremer

1001 Ways to Market Your Books
Digital World Series

Open Horizons
P. O. Box 2887
Taos NM 87571
575-751-3398

Email: JohnKremer@BookMarket.com

Web: https://www.BookMarketingBestsellers.com

Introduction

There are two major ways to market books and authors in today's world: 1. Speak, and 2. Drive online traffic to your books and websites.

Speaking

Speak live wherever any one will invite you or welcome you. For authors, speak at bookstores and libraries most of all. But also speak at Rotary Clubs, Lions Clubs, garden clubs, churches, schools, colleges, cruise ships, museums, bars, donut shops, senior citizen centers, Jaycees, chambers of commerce, hospitals, conferences, adult learning centers, professional meetings, and anywhere else that welcomes speakers and entertainers.

Do media interviews, not just on radio and TV, but also for newspapers and magazines. Focus on two levels of media: local and national. Local media should welcome you as a local celebrity, but national media will really up your exposure and your credibility.

Please note: National TV shows are hungry for new experts who can provide great sound bites when commenting on the latest news and events.

Get interviewed online. Online interviews are an incredible way to get exposure online and traffic to your website. Work to get invited on podcasts, Facebook Live events, YouTube Live videos, webinars, teleseminars, Skype interviews, and telesummits.

In another book in this Digital World Series, I will provide details on how to book online interviews and how to sell your books and services via those interviews.

Drive Online Traffic

The key to success in marketing on the Internet is to get meaningful traffic to your web pages, especially those pages that feature your book for sale, your course for sale, your membership site for sale, or your other products and services for sale.

There are four major ways to get targeted traffic to your websites, email capture pages, or sales pages.

1. Pay for it. Buy and test advertisements on Facebook, Google Search, Bing Search, Amazon (via Amazon Marketing Services), and other social media ads.

The key to advertising is to start small and test everything (target audience, the wording of the ads, the venues for the ads, etc.). Keep testing until you find ads that work. That means the ad brings in more income than it costs. Once you find such working ads, keep running them for as long as they keep working.

2. Partner with others. You can also get traffic by working with other influencers to drive traffic. With most partnerships, you give a piece of the action to encourage your partners to send you more traffic via product launches, webinars, teleseminars, podcasts, telesummits, and more. The best kind of partnership is a joint venture where your partners benefit monetarily for sending you buying traffic.

I'll be writing a book about online advertising and online partnerships as part of the Digital World Series. It might take awhile for me to complete the book, but it will come out within the next year at the latest.

3. Own your keywords online. My next book in the Digital World Series for *1001 Ways to Market Your Books* will be a book on how to own your keywords and topics online. There are an incredible number of ways for you to start to own your keywords and topics in a meaningful way that sends you targeted buying traffic. I will be covering those ways in the new book.

4. Use content to optimize search engine visibility. Search engines are still responsible for more than half of all traffic that comes to most websites. You want to create lots of content so your website, landing pages, blog posts, and sales pages all show up in the key search engines.

The key search engines besides Google and Bing are Amazon, YouTube, Pinterest, and other social media networks. The more content you create, the more visible you and your books, products, or services will become.

90% of the traffic to my websites comes from two sources: SEO based on content and Pinterest pins.

This book is all about content. It provides you with 105 key pieces of content that you can create to draw more people to come to your website—and come to your website over and over again.

Of course, you don't just want any old kind of traffic. You want targeted traffic from people who love the kind of content you create and who are willing to pay for it by buying your books, products, and/or services.

This book is about personal blogging for authors, experts, and plain old people. The next book in the series will be about content marketing in a really serious way. In that book, we will cover incredible ways to use content marketing to build targeted traffic, get more search engine visibility, and make more sales.

But, now, let's talk about personal blogging for authors and experts.

Personal Blogging Ideas . . .

This book is all about creating content that pulls in targeted traffic from the people you really want to reach with your core message. Great content draws in the people you want to reach.

We all know that blogging is one of the best ways to get attention in today's internet world. A blog is a godsend to your website, bringing it targeted traffic, dedicated fans, and ready buyers.

A blog also is an easy way to create more and more pages on your website, thus making your website more visible to the search engines. But, to get that organic traffic, you have to post regularly: twice a week or more.

Ideally, if you want to build up a large audience for your website, get more subscribers for your newsletter, and encourage more readers of your blog, you should post every work day (that's Monday through Friday during most weeks).

Stuck for what to blog about? What kind of content should you feature?

Here are some tips that I originally wrote for novelists, but the same tips (revised and updated) can apply to writers of nonfiction books, memoirs, children's books, business books, poetry, novels, and more.

These tips can also apply to anyone marketing products or services online, no matter what kind of product, no matter what kind of service, no matter the audience, no matter where you live.

So, check out the kind of content you can create—and take action by writing a new blog post or website article every day.

Of course, you should also use these same ideas for tweets, pins, Facebook posts, LinkedIn posts, podcasts, videos, audios, article ideas, press releases, book ideas, speech ideas, and more.

So get cracking!

1. Review other novels, books, or ebooks in your field.

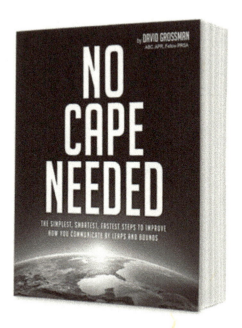

The best books to reviews are those from lesser-known novelists or book authors in your field. These relatively unknown authors will become your friends and fans fast because you reviewed their books. In turn, they will blog about you, review your ebook, or add a link to your review of their books.

Check out this promo review for *No Cape Needed*: https://bookmarketingbestsellers.com/booksellers-recommend-david-grossmans-no-cape-needed.

2. Write a blog post using the voice of one of your main characters.

For nonfiction authors, write a blog post using the voice of Abraham Lincoln, Gandhi, Plato, Teddy Roosevelt, Dr. Oz, Henry David Thoreau, Oprah Winfrey, Bob Villa, Howard Cosell, or some other famous person in your field.

Here's an example from The Blog of Henry David Thoreau at https://blogthoreau.blogspot.com/2014/08/i-cannot-spare-my-moonlight-thoreaus.html

I cannot spare my moonlight

...Thoreau Journal: 02-Aug-1854

My attic chamber has compelled me to sit below with the family at evening for a month. I feel the necessity of deepening the stream of my life; I must cultivate privacy. It is very dissipating to be with people too much. As C. says, it takes the edge off a man's thoughts to have been too much in society. I cannot spare my moonlight and my mountains for the best of man I am likely to get in exchange.

3. Tell stories.

Have that main character tell some side stories not included in the novel or which are actually side stories within the novel itself.

For nonfiction authors, you can tell stories you did not feature in your book. Or expand upon the stories you told in your book.

Here's an example from Aaron Shapiro, author of *Users Not Customers* (AaronShapiro.com):

Here's what Borders did wrong. Borders was years late to sell books online. When it did, it outsourced the project to one of its chief competitors, Amazon. At the start of 2011, after the company took back control of its Internet operations, online hardcopy sales accounted for less than 3 percent of Borders' revenue—that's less than a third of what Barnes & Noble derived from its online hardcopy sales. Then to add insult to injury, it was also late on the e-book craze, creating a me-too e-reader almost three years after Amazon introduced the Kindle.

4. Write about the setting – the time and/or place.

For novelists, use some of the research you did to ensure that your novel was accurate. Offer additional information on the time or place where your novel is set. Readers of novels love such added details about the novel's setting.

Nonfiction authors can write about the time, place, or setting that inspired them to write their ebooks. Where or when did you get the idea for your ebook in the first place?

Here's a post on my Book Marketing Bestsellers blog where I wrote about the genesis for this book (when it was simply called *101 Ways to Blog as an Ebook Author*): https://openhorizons.blogspot.com/2011/11/book-authors-perennial-question-where.html.

One question authors get asked a lot is: Where Do You Get Your Ideas?

*Well, here's where I got my idea for a new Kindle ebook, **101 Ways to Blog as a Book Author**. I got the idea earlier this evening while listening to Ty Cohen present his Kindle Cash Flow webinar.*

*I thought: Why not turn some of my blog posts into books? One of my longest blog posts is one I did on **101 Ways to Blog as a Book Author**. That, in turn, was inspired by another blog post I did in response to something I saw on Ezine Articles: **45 Ways to Blog as a Novelist: Tips for Writers of Fiction**.*

I've been asked many times by ebook authors to write some books specifically on how to market ebooks. During Ty's webinar, I realized I should do that. I'll be writing several such books, but I thought I'd start with one that is half-written: 101 Ways to Blog as a eBook Author.

5. Invite your readers to review your book.

Write a blog post asking visitors to review your ebook. You might offer your ebook at a discount in return for the reader's commitment to writing and posting a review.

Here's a request I made while writing an article on the importance of testimonials, a key to book marketing: https://bookmarketingbestsellers.com/testimonials-one-of-the-keys-to-book-marketing.

Testimonials can make a difference in how people see your book. Work to get some great ones. Ask the experts in the field. Ask those who buy your book ahead of time. Ask your online friends. Ask your social media followers.

Great testimonials can sell great books!

Here are some of the great testimonials I've received for my book, 1001 Ways to Market Your Books. I'm always looking for more. You can email me yours via books@bookmarketingbestsellers.com. Thanks!

6. Feature reader testimonials on your blog.

I created a John Kremer Fan Club to feature some of the great testimonials I've received over the years. Here's one such testimonial from Susan Zimmer, author of *I Love Coffee*: https://bookmarketingbestsellers.com/john-kremer-fan-club-susan-zimmer-author-of-i-love-coffee

"*1001 Ways to Market Your Books* is a ship of great thoughts and ideas. It's been my bible to successfully sell 50,000 copies (40,000 in English and 10,000 in French) of my first self-published book in just over 4 years! I took my passion, poured it into a unique coffee gift book and served it via *1001 Ways* to generate a demand and attract the world's largest gift book publisher. If I can do it, anyone can — using *1001 Ways*."

Susan Zimmer, author, *I Love Coffee!*

I love coffee! Over 100 Easy and Delicious Coffee Drinks

"IF YOU WANT TO SELL 650,000,000 BOOKS LIKE WE HAVE, READ AND USE THIS BOOK."

1001 Ways to Market Your Books

Real World Edition

JOHN KREMER

http://amzn.to/2BeKUxr

BookMarketingBestsellers.com

7. Interview some of your readers.

You can interview others via Q&A text, via an Internet radio show, via a teleseminar, via a Facebook Live, via a YouTube Live, via Zoom, via Skype. You have many many options in today's world of the Internet to interview others.

Master marketer Jay Abraham has created hundreds of relationships with highly successful business and thought leaders. In this segment he interviews Brian Tracy, a noted author, seminar leader and professional speaker with Hall of Fame status.

Watch here: https://bookmarketingbestsellers.com/jay-abraham-interviews-brian-tracy.

8. Feature an interview of you.

In your blog post, feature an interview of you where someone else asked the questions and you gave the answers. That interview, again, can be in written format, in audio format, or in video format.

Here's a written interview of me that I posted a number of years ago on my old blog (the answers still have value): https://openhorizons.blogspot.com/2006/03/interview-with-john-kremer.html:

Here's an excerpt from a short interview I did the other day:

__1. Why should individuals consider marketing__ to be such a high priority (whether it's to sell more copies or reach more readers and educate them or entertain them)?

__John's Answer:__ Marketing is a high priority for only one reason. That's how you reach potential readers of your books— and why would you write if you didn't want readers?

__2. What types of people might be suited to self-publish__ or to control a great part of their marketing destiny even if they are traditionally published?

John's Answer: *Entrepreneurial people, plain and simple. Don't self-publish if you don't want to take control of your own destiny in publishing and writing books. You must be willing to spend time doing much of the promotion yourself rather than paying someone else to do it.*

3. What is the importance of people, *especially everyday ones, writing a book in their lifetime?*

John's Answer: *There is no importance to anyone writing a book unless they have to write one. Writing one simply because it's fashionable or the thing to do will result in a lousy book. But, if you can't help yourself, if you must write, if you must put what you know and feel into a book, if you are passionate about what you are writing, then it is important to write.*

4. What excites you *about working in the publishing industry/working with authors?*

John's Answer: *I love great book ideas, great book execution, great book reading experiences. When an author is passionate about her work, then I'm interested. Then I get excited.*

9. Podcast your book, one section at a time.

Or do a video podcast in the same way. Or, better yet, do both. Once you've created a video podcast, an audio podcast is easy to create by simply reproducing the audio portion of the video.

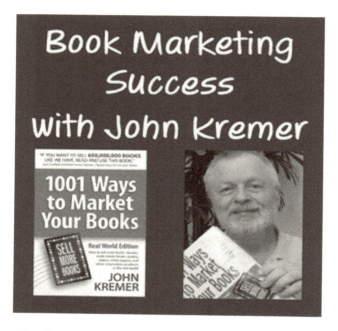

Check out John Kremer's Book Marketing Success Podcast series I created a few years ago: https://bookmarketingbestsellers.com/book-marketing-success-podcast.

Below are the notes from one of the podcast segments (https://bookmarketingbestsellers.com/book-marketing-success-stories-do-you-hate-to-market-books).

If they are truly honest, all authors hate marketing. They'd rather write.

Building relationships is the key to marketing. And that's just a matter of making friends.

Of course, if you write a great book, your marketing is at least half done. Great books create great fans. And great fans sell books.

Remember: 80% of all books are sold by word of mouth. Your job is to get that word of mouth started by writing a great book and then marketing your book every day.

Rely on the relationships you've created with other book authors, with readers, with fans, with the people that read your blog, and with any joint venture partners.

10. Write about trends in your genre or subject area.

You can create a Google alert to keep you updated on the latest news, statistics, blog posts, etc. so you have something to write about.

Below, for example, is a blog post (video and text) covering a few facts and statistics on content marketing: https://bookmarketingbestsellers.com/content-marketing-video-facts-and-statistics-on-content-marketing.

Infographic Marketing: Users are 30 times more likely to read an infographic than an article. Infographics are shared on social media 3 times more than other content. Infographics generate 45% more search volume than other types of content.

Blogging: 45% of marketers believe that blogging is the most important content strategy they can employ for developing their business. 30% of the two million blog posts published every day are list articles. Content with images get up to 94% more views.

Video Marketing: *Videos make it 50 times easier to become ranked on the first page of Google. Videos drive a 157% increase in organic traffic. 74% of all traffic in 2017 will be video.*

Email Marketing: *204 million email messages are sent every minute of every day. Email is 40 times more effective at acquiring new paying customers than Twitter or Facebook. Use the word video in your email subject line. That boosts open rates by 19%, increases click-through rates by 65%, and reduces unsubscribes by 26%.*

Social Media Marketing: *The top four social media platforms for content marketing are Facebook, Twitter, YouTube, and LinkedIn. 500 million people watch a Facebook video every day.*

11. Write about your favorite book authors.

For novelists, write about your favorite novelists, especially those that write in your genre.

For nonfiction authors, write about book authors in your field. Include their photos and a sampling of their books. And, of course, you can link to their books for sale on Amazon via an affiliate link.

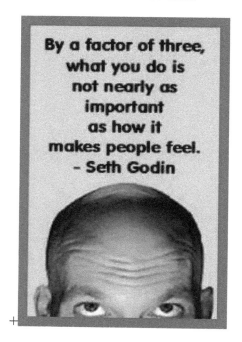

On my Book Marketing Bestsellers website, I've written about Seth Godin many times. I love his work, and I love to share it with others. On the next few pages are a few sample blog posts featuring Seth.

Note: Seth has given me permission to reprint his material any time.

Seth Godin: Books Matter - https://bookmarketingbestsellers.com/seth-godin-books-matter

Seth Godin: 5 Book Marketing Tips for Book Authors - https://bookmarketingbestsellers.com/seth-godin-5-book-marketing-tips-for-book-authors

Seth Godin: On Books, Blogs, and Tribes - https://bookmarketingbestsellers.com/seth-godin-on-books-blogs-and-tribes (a podcast featuring Seth Godin)

Seth Godin: 19 Points of Advice for Book Authors - https://bookmarketingbestsellers.com/seth-godin-19-points-of-advice-for-book-authors

Seth Godin: How to Sell a Book or Any New Idea - https://bookmarketingbestsellers.com/seth-godin-how-to-sell-a-book-or-any-new-idea (an excerpt from a manifesto written by Seth)

Seth Godin: On Finding Customers - https://bookmarketingbestsellers.com/seth-godin-on-finding-customers (a quote from Seth, short and sweet)

Seth Godin: Pick Yourself - https://bookmarketingbestsellers.com/seth-godin-pick-yourself (another quote from Seth: *No one is going to pick you. Pick yourself.*)

Seth Godin on How You Make People Feel - https://bookmarketingbestsellers.com/seth-godin-on-how-you-make-people-feel

Seth Godin: How Much Should an Ebook Cost? - http://bookmarketingbestsellers.com/seth-godin-how-much-should-an-ebook-cost

Seth Godin: Harper Lee and Two Mythical Promises - http://bookmarketingbestsellers.com/seth-godin-harper-lee-and-two-mythical-promises

Seth Godin on Horizontal Book Launches - https://bookmarketingbestsellers.com/seth-godin-on-horizontal-book-launches

I've explored a variety of ways to get to market with the books I've created over the last thirty years. I've self-published, worked with most of the major NY publishing houses, did a partnership with Barnes and Noble and another with Amazon—all as a way to solve the problem of discovery. How do we get books into the hands of people who want to read them?

Horizontal Book Launches

Seth Godin

Ask your core fans to pre-order multiple copies of your new book.

Offer your fans a big discount for the first exclusive print run.

Make that first print run a big deal — an exclusive deal just for them.

Your first readers will become passionate distributors for your book.

Fans will hand-sell your book to friends, colleagues, and members of their tribe.

Fans will use your book to teach and inspire.

Horizontal movement — side to side, person to person — not top down.

That's a horizontal book launch!

Seth Godin on Book Covers - https://bookmarketingbestsellers.com/seth-godin-on-book-covers

Seth Godin on a Good Day's Work - https://bookmarketingbestsellers.com/seth-godin-on-a-good-days-work

Seth Godin on The Bestseller Effect - https://bookmarketingbestsellers.com/seth-godin-on-the-bestseller-effect

> **Bestsellers are the books that people who don't buy books are buying.**
> **— Seth Godin**

12. Answer questions from your readers.

On my Book Marketing Bestsellers website, I now offer people the opportunity to ask me a question

If you had a chance to ask John Kremer, a 35-year book marketing veteran, anything about getting more traffic, getting more leads, making more book sales, social media ins & outs, or other book marketing questions, self-publishing questions, or book publishing questions, what's the #1 question you'd ask him?

There is no charge to ask a question. I will answer any and all appropriate questions here on this website. Watch for my answers!

Ask your Book Marketing Question below . . .

Name

First	Last

Email

Subject

Message

Submit Your Question

You can ask your question here: https://bookmarketingbestsellers.com/book-marketing-qa-with-john-kremer-ask-your-questions-here.

13. Fill in the back stories of some of your minor characters.

For novelists, you can tell the back story of one or more of your minor characters. For instance, Diana Gabaldon, author of *The Outlander* series has written a number of novelettes featuring Lord John, a wonderfully quirky character that many readers have fallen in love with.

For nonfiction authors, you can write about a back story featuring one of the stories, facts, or statistics you shared in your book.

Here's a story I shared on an experience that built upon the latest edition of *1001 Ways to Market Your Books*:

I recently returned from a conference in California and wore a t-shirt with my 1001 Ways to Market Your Books cover. I got a comment on the shirt from someone in the elevator going down to catch the shuttle van, from someone at the front desk, from two people in the shuttle van who needed the book (I referred them to my BookMarket.com website), another person in the van, the person at the check-in counter, someone in line to board the plane, the pilot when getting off the plane, and someone in the grocery store on the way home.

Not bad for an $18.00 t-shirt from CafePress.com.

More than one person commented: I guess that's 1002 ways to market your books (the t-shirt being the extra way). Of course, the truth is that t-shirts are already included in the 1001, but I just agreed. It's simpler that way.

14. Write a new short story.

Feature one of the minor characters in your novel. Again, you could even create a collection of short stories built around your novels, as Diana Gabaldon has done.

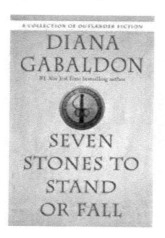

For nonfiction authors, you could write a funny story about a co-author, illustrator, or interviewee who contributed to your book.

Or you could simply learn how to tell great stories, and then tell some via your blog posts.

15. Feature excerpts from your upcoming novels or books.

Feature excerpts from your novels, nonfiction books, or speeches you give. Be sure to ask for feedback with any free excerpts you give away as blog posts or free ebooks.

The following is a post I wrote for my old Book Promotion blog. It's excerpted from a seminar I presented in Singapore for the Singapore Book Publishers Association. (https://openhorizons.blogspot.com/2011/10/top-4-book-marketing-tactics-in-todays.html).

The Top 4 Book Marketing Tactics in Today's World

Here are the top four book promotion activities you can engage in to sell more books in today's world . . .

1. Speak. Speaking builds a word-of-mouth army better than anything else. Speak locally - at garden clubs, libraries, bookstores, Rotary clubs, JCs, poetry nights, story swaps, book club meetings, etc. Then expand out to a wider area, to nearby cities, to nearby states. Eventually, expand out to an even wider audience.

When someone hears you speak, they become a bigger fan than if they had just read your book. If they like you when they hear you speak, they will tell ten times more people than by just reading your book.

2. Book yourself on national TV. *TV is still the largest mass market media. It still reaches more people than any other media - and with more impact. It's worth spending the time contacting the ten or twenty news and talk shows that reach your audience. For most national TV shows, you can get the contact information in one of two ways: 1. from their websites, and 2. via your network of friends and fellow authors.*

Your appearance on one major TV show will not only expose you to millions of viewers, but it also opens the door to dozens and sometimes hundreds of other media: newspapers, magazines, radio, more TV shows, etc.

3. Create relationships with high-traffic websites. *How many major high-traffic websites that attract your target reader have you created relationships with? Are these real relationships where you contribute content to them on a regular basis? In today's world, Internet relationships are the key to marketing success.*

Uncover five to ten top websites that already reach the audience you want to reach. Look over their sites until you find a way to contact someone behind the site - a webmaster, an editor, the founder. Then email them with an offer of free content for their readers: an interview with you, a review copy of your book, a free article (that is really good), some tips for their readers, a Q&A column on *your specialty, etc. Their obligation, in return, is to link to your website or sales page.*

4. Do a Superstar Blog Tour. *Or a Mega Blog Tour. Or a Blogpalooza. I'm not talking about the old-style humdrum virtual book tour of 15 or 20 blogs. I'm talking about an event blog tour that creates Internet buzz on a major scale. Event blog tours can build brands, create incredible website traffic, and sell tons of books.*

The neat thing is that effective event blog tours take less time to carry out than the traditional Amazon Bestseller Campaign - and are almost always more effective in selling books, building a brand, and driving traffic.

16. Excerpt from other people's blogs.

You can always excerpt from other people's blog posts, websites, or social media posts. When you excerpt some content from another person's blog or website, be sure to comment on that excerpt. And always link back to the original source.

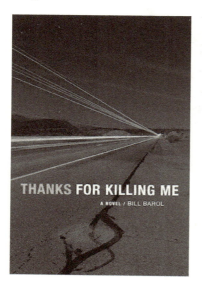

Here's an excerpt from a post I did for my old Book Promotion blog (excerpting content from Bill's blog post): https://openhorizons.blogspot.com/2011/10/book-promotion-via-giving-away-books.html.

Bill Barol, author of the crime caper novel Thanks for Killing Me, *is conducting an experiment in book promotion. He self-published his novel via CreateSpace and, after discussing his book promotion with a publishing friend, decided to give his book away (or, at least, sell it for as low a price as he could, given his relationship with CreateSpace).*

As his publishing friend advised him, "First, forget everything you know about traditional media; all your experience is worthless. Take all that time you spend screwing around on Twitter and put it into marketing your book. And, at least in the beginning, sell it as cheap as you can. In fact, you know what? Give it away."

As Bill noted in a blog post about his adventures in self-publishing:

His reasoning was hard to argue with, and not just because I suddenly had a loud buzzing in my ears and the room was all swimmy. The logic went like this: Given two facts—the odds of any self-published novel ever making any real dough were astronomically low, and the job of my novel was now to be its own loss leader—why not set its retail valuation at zero and get it into as many hands as possible?

It sounded screwy, it sounded counter-intuitive—hell, it was counter-intuitive, as my intuition was to make money by my work, and as much of it as possible. But the more I thought about it the less nuts it sounded. If I was really serious about exposing my work to a broad audience and generating the kind of critical mass that would make publishers reconsider, I had to make the book almost impossible for anyone with even a passing interest not to acquire.

The Get It/Don't Get It decision had to be friction-free, and cost was the point of friction I could most easily lubricate.

boingboing / BILL BAROL

To read more about his decision and how he priced his book to sell cheap, see *Adventures in self-publishing: Why I took a year's work and tried my hardest to give it away* - https://boingboing.net/2011/10/17/adventures.html.

17. Link to the blogs of your favorite authors.

Tell readers why those blogs would interest them.

As noted in an earlier point, I've linked to many blog posts from Seth Godin, one of my favorite book authors and also one of my favorite bloggers.

In another post, I linked to top do-it-yourself bloggers, food bloggers, beauty and fashion bloggers, garden bloggers, and more: https://bookmarketingbestsellers.com/diy-bloggers-food-bloggers-beauty-bloggers-garden-bloggers.

18. Link to book review sites.

Recommend your favorite book review sites, book bloggers, and other book reviewers.

Linking to other top sites helps you to create relationships with those sites.

It also, of course, helps your SEO (search engine optimization) since high-quality links to other top websites is one way that search engines measure quality websites.

And, finally, such useful quality links help the people who visit your site. That gets your site more word of mouth.

On the Book Marketing Bestsellers website, I feature many top newspaper book reviewers: https://bookmarketingbestsellers.com/newspaper-book-review-editors.

19. Create a hall of fame for your genre or topic.

Of course, include yourself in any hall of fame you create.

Here is the newest iteration of my Self-Publishing Hall of Fame: https://bookmarketingbestsellers.com/self-publishing-hall-of-fame.

Will Bowen: To Market Your Book, Start a Movement

Dallas Clayton: An Awesome World of Book Marketing

Colleen Hoover: A New York Times Bestselling Self-Published Novelist

Dawn Ireland: On Postcard Marketing

Carla King and the World of Motorcycling

Michael J. Knowles: #1 Bestselling Blank Book

Jim Misko: How to Do a Statewide Book Tour for Your Novel

Boyd Morrison: On Writing Thrillers and Self-Publishing

Neil Ostroff: On Marketing Books Via the Internet

John Penberthy: How to Sell $40,000 in Foreign Rights

Diane Pfeifer: On Selling a Million Books a Year

Derek Walcott: Nobel Prize-Winning Poet and Playwright

Andy Weir: How to Create a Bestselling Novel (and Movie)!

Milo Yiannopoulos: Self-Publisher of Dangerous Milo

Ernie Zelinski: Creative Book Marketing Strategies

20. Feature events.

Write a blog post or feature article for each of your upcoming book signing events, online events, seminars, webinars, teleseminars, talks, etc. Invite your readers to attend and encourage them to let their friends know about your events.

I did a discount promotion for Nanowrimo (National Novel Writing Month) in November 2018 for my Book Title Critique Service. You can read about my offer here: https://bookmarketingbestsellers.com/book-title-critiques.

An effective book title alone can make the difference between a mediocre seller and a bestselling book.

The title of a book, like the headline of an advertisement or news story, often makes the difference between a reader passing the book by or picking it up and giving it more careful consideration.

More often than not, the reader gives less than a moment's attention to any book title; if you don't capture the reader's imagination or curiosity or desire in that short moment, you will have lost the sale.

More important, however, is that many distributors, bookstore buyers, reviewers, and subsidiary rights buyers also judge a book by its title (and its cover). They know from experience that a good title sells more books.

21. Write a follow-up post on each of your events.

After you've done an event, you can write a follow-up blog post or article where you describe what happened at the event. Also take photos of the event and post them in the blog post as well.

Recently I created a video for a self-published book author. David Parker, author of _The More You Do The Better You Feel: How to Overcome Procrastination and Live a Happier Life_, has taken over a thousand photos of people who have bought his book directly from him at various events and shows. In the video, I showcased about 20 of those people. It was a fun video to create.

You, too, can start to collect photos of people who have bought your book. Just ask! And get their permission to share their photo on your website, via social media, or in other promotions. Get their permission in writing (bring along permission forms when you sell your books at live events).

Then showcase those people in your blog posts, social media, a page on your website, or videos you upload to YouTube, Facebook, Twitter, etc.

Here's the blog post I wrote for the video I created for David: https://bookmarketingbestsellers.com/people-love-a-book-video.

And the video tweet I created for the video as well: https://twitter.com/JohnKremer/status/1065538609107718145.

And the Facebook post for the video: https://www.facebook.com/johnkremer/posts/10156883829539553.

And the pin I posted on Pinterest: https://www.pinterest.com/pin/57983913938375609.

And the YouTube video upload: https://www.youtube.com/watch?v=lUFn34uv0Uk

Those are just a few of the online places where you can save a short video that you have created from your event.

22. Review book trailers for books you like.

You can review video trailers for books you don't like. Then feature the book trailer video in a blog post, on your website, and via your social media profiles.

Check out my review and commentary on a book trailer for Jennifer Belle's novel The Seven Year Bitch. It's an incredibly easy book trailer any author could duplicate: https://bookmarketingbestsellers.com/fun-viral-book-trailer-incredibly-easy-to-duplicate-for-any-book.

The video features various women reading the novel and loving it—laughing and laughing and laughing. Doesn't this make you want to read Jennifer's novel as well?

You can easily create a similar trailer for your book. Just gather a few friends around your home. Give them a copy of your book. Point them to a page where your book is really funny, or really sad, or really moving. Have them start reading. Then record their reactions.

Pick the best reactions to feature in your new video.

Of course, be sure to get a signed model release that gives you permission to use their images and reactions in a video you upload to YouTube, other social networks, and your website.

Why not make a viral video today?

If you do create such a video, let me know (email: books@bookmarketingbestsellers.com. I'll post your video on my Book Marketing Bestsellers website.

23. Write about your work routine.

As a book author, you can describe when you write (morning, evening, weekends, before work), where you write (the proverbial garret, in a coffee shop, at the kitchen table), and how you prepare to write (eat a banana, listen to music, kick your husband or wife out of the house). You could easily stretch this description of your writing routine out into three or four short blog posts.

If you are not a book author, you can describe your work routine for your job, your hobby, your entrepreneurial odd job, etc.

Here's a blog post that Leo Babauta of ZenHabits wrote about writing (https://www.zenhabits.net/writer). He included one key tip on his writing routine.

You should care about writing. I'll tell you why: It's an incredible tool for learning about yourself. And if you're an effective writer, you're an effective communicator, thinker, salesperson, businessperson, persuader.

1. Write every damn day.

Yes, even weekends. Yes, even when you're busy with other crap. Each day I write a blog post, an article for Sea Change, part of my new book, or perhaps part of a novel.

If I don't have enough to write every day, I start a new writing project. I write at least 1,000 words a day, but you don't have to write that much.

Writing daily makes it a routine thing, so you never have to think about it. You just do it. It gets much easier, less intimidating. You get better at it. It's like talking with a friend: just how you express yourself.

Leo Babauta

14 Observations on Writing

1. Write every damn day.
2. Create a blog if you have none.
3. Write plainly.
4. Don't write just to hear yourself talk.
5. Nearly everything can be shorter.
6. Fear stops most potential writers.
7. Read regularly for inspiration.
8. Procrastination is your friend.
9. Have people expect your writing.
10. Email is an excuse.
11. Writing tools don't matter.
12. Jealousy is idiotic.
13. Writing can change lives.
14. Writing changes you.

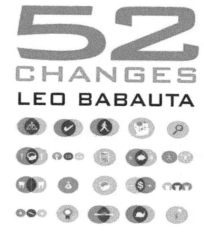

BookMarketingBestsellers.com

24. Share the genesis of your book.

Blog about your book or novel. How did it come about? What ideas, events, characters, etc. inspired you to write the book?

Check out this video post on telling stories, which features why I wrote *1001 Ways to Market Your Books*. In essence, I tell a story to showcase the power of telling stories!

https://bookmarketingbestsellers.com/become-a-storyteller-if-you-want-to-sell-more-books.

Author Marketing Tip: Tell a story. All marketing, ultimately, is about telling stories. Become a storyteller if you want to sell more copies of your books.

25. Give an inside look.

For novelists, describe how you went about plotting your novel or developing the characters.

For nonfiction authors, describe how you went about organizing the book, why you included some things and excluded other info.

In a Skype interview I did a few months ago with Bevan Atkinson, author of _The Tarot Mysteries_ series, she talked about how she listened to the characters in her novels as she writes them.

You can watch the Skype interview here: https://bookmarketingbestsellers.com/bevan-atkinson-how-to-listen-to-voices-when-writing.

26. Write about a hobby you have.

On my Book Marketing Bestsellers website, I often share my hobbies (in the form of the websites where I feature them):

http://www.MyIncredibleWebsite.com

http://www.CelebrityWeightLossTips.com

27. Write about a cause that's important to you.

It can be any cause that you are passionate about: charitable, political, social, ecological, or spiritual.

Here's an excerpt from a post I wrote for my old Book Promotion blog that was inspired by a Seth Godin post: https://openhorizons.blogspot.com/2006/11/polite-fictions-and-true-cause-related.html.

Polite Fictions and True Cause-Related Marketing

In his blog today, Seth Godin writes about polite fictions, where everyone agrees to a story so they can go on doing what they are doing.

For instance, many of us like Ben & Jerry's ice cream so we applaud them for all their cleverness and devotion to social causes. But the truth is that ice cream is really bad for us, especially eating too much of it. Eating Ben & Jerry's (or other ice cream) can lead to being overweight, getting diabetes, developing heart disease, etc. But with Ben & Jerry's, as compared to many other ice cream brands, we can feel somewhat good about it because Ben and Jerry are so nice.

Now, if Ben & Jerry really wanted to do some good, they would lead the fight against heart disease (which, if they were honest with themselves, they might actually have a hand in creating).

If they were to embrace true cause-related marketing, they'd get behind and support heart disease research—AND they would encourage people to eat their ice cream in moderation. They would create an entire campaign encouraging people to watch what they eat. It's hard for them to condemn McDonalds (I don't know if they do) when they are selling high-fat, high-calorie ice cream that can do as much damage as eating at McDonalds.

Of course, with the polite fiction that many of us participate in, we can feel much better about eating Ben & Jerry's than eating at McDonalds. That's why a man can make a movie about McDonalds (Super Size Me) but I doubt anyone would make a similar movie about Ben & Jerry's. They're some of the good guys, while McDonalds is simply a big, evil corporation.

The truth is that both foods are terrible for us in excess, but probably okay in moderation. But try telling that to people who attack McDonalds while happily eating their Ben & Jerry's. Polite fictions, they are a way of life.

What polite fictions are you living with? What have you agreed to ignore?

How does this all relate to book marketing? Well, if you're going to get involved in cause-related marketing, make sure that the causes you support are ones you can live with, ones that lessen the damage you do to your body, your environment, or your society.

For instance, I believe that book publishers and authors should support associations that help to reforest our land or preserve the wild areas that are left. Why? Because books use a lot of paper—and that, right now, means lots of trees. Until we as a society begin using hemp for paper, book authors and publishers need to support reforestation and nature preservation.

28. Write about your family.

If you want to be a real person in the eyes of your readers or customers, sometimes you should write about your spouse, your children, or other members of your family.

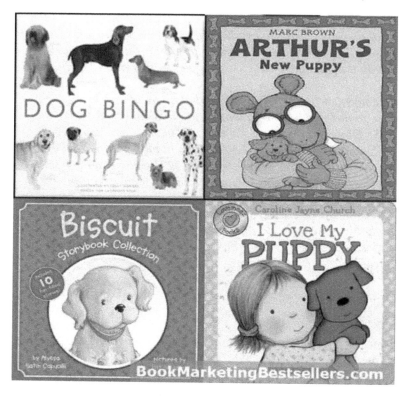

Here is a post I did on the top dog books for children: https://bookmarketingbestsellers.com/the-top-dog-books-for-children.

My wife and I have two dogs that we love very much. Becky is our older dog. She's a wonderful dog, but often fearful when meeting new people, so she nips at their heels. Poe is our younger dog. He's so sweet. He loves everyone and every dog. Both are rescue dogs.

29. Write about where you live.

You can write about your town, your state, your country, your world, or your galaxy. Make it personal. Tell your story in the context of where you live. You story can be fun, personal, serious, or simply the facts.

Here's a Facebook post I shared recently at https://www.facebook.com/johnkremer:

Had to dig out of the deep snow today just to open my front door—here on the side of a mountain outside Taos, New Mexico. Now warm sunny skies after a night of constant snow.

The grocery store in Taos, New Mexico where I do most of my food shopping.

Of course, you could write about more important issues: social, political, economic, educational, etc. Or something more lighthearted: a travelogue, interesting local people, something in your town that you are proud of.

Recently, I shared a photo of my favorite grocery store in Taos, a store that features lots of natural, organic, and local produce and foods.

Check out the photo on Facebook or on the previous page: https://www.facebook.com/johnkremer/posts/10156806083954553.

30. State your opinion on the state of the world.

Share your opinion on politics, the nation, the world, the environment, or other social causes.

Here's a tweet I shared a number of years ago at https://twitter.com/johnkremer. My tweet generated quite a controversy:

> *Free speech is still alive in book publishing. Fantastic - Glenn Beck earned $13 million last year from book publishing.*

I responded with a note in my *Book Marketing Tip of the Week* email newsletter:

I received a number of tweets freaking out that I mentioned Glenn Beck in a tweet—even though the tweet was focused on his success in writing books. I thought the tweet focused on two good points about the news story this tweet came from: 1. Free speech is alive in book publishing. We publish all points of view. 2. Books are still making money.

One person wrote: BECK - YIKES - this scares me.

Another wrote: John - that's a scary commentary.

Why does this scare people? Have they ever watched Glenn Beck's TV show? I've been watching Beck for the past few weeks, and he is one of the most reasonable people on TV or radio. I don't know how he is on his radio show, but his TV show covers a lot of history, reasonable arguments, and very few rants (some guilt by association).

I find Glenn a lot easier to listen to than Randi Rhodes, who yells at her listeners every day, cuts them off, tries to talk over them. Ed Schultz does the same thing. I like Thom Hartmann a whole lot better. And miss Ron Reagan. All four are or were radio hosts featured on KVOT (the local Taos progressive radio station).

I'm all for free speech. And I encourage anyone to listen to all points of view and not shut out people simply because they are accused of bias or extremism. Judge for yourself by really listening.

31. Comment on scandals.

Write about Harvey Weinstein, Matt Lauer, Mark Halperin, Michael Avenatti, Les Moonves, Gil Cisneros, and other fools. There's a new one born every day in the news. Comment on the #metoo movement, #timesup, #imwithher, sexual predation, abuse of power, etc.

I created a post blessing all the victims of rape, etc.: http://myincrediblewebsite.com/god-bless-the-victims.

God bless the victims of rape, sexual assault, sexual harassment, sexual predation, sexual misconduct, sexual misbehavior, and abuse of power. It's sad that this list is so long.

You're nothing. We're everything.

32. Write about a hot issue or current news item.

Write about issues or news, especially something that relates to your novel or book.

When Steve Jobs died, I shared a viral video that featured great quotes from him on following your heart, staying hungry, staying foolish, and never settling—themes I share often in my books and blogs.

In another post, I shared the following image (http://myincrediblewebsite.com/steve-jobs-double-perspective-illusion):

In honor of Steve Jobs, someone created the following double perspective illusion. I'm not sure who created it but I wanted to share it.

This double perspective illusion can be seen as a bite out of an apple – or as Steve Jobs's shadow profile over the Apple logo.

33. Describe how you go about doing research for your book.

Do you read other books? Use Google? Check out related websites? Travel places? Read blogs? Use Wikipedia? Ask your readers? Query your social network followers? Write about that.

In a Book Marketing Bestsellers post on Advice to Would-Be Book Authors, I offered the following tips on how to research books: https://bookmarketingbestsellers.com/john-kremers-advice-to-would-be-book-authors.

For authors who want to write a book but do not yet know how to go about it and don't quite know how to get started —the desire is enough. If you have a passion for your topic and for your book, you can write a book. Start simply.

If you are writing a novel, then read good novels in your genre (romance, mysteries, fantasy, etc.). Read some of the classics as well as some more recent fiction. Get to know the history and current style of the genre you want to write.

Similarly, if you are working on a nonfiction book, read bestselling or highly recommended books on your specific topic. Again, read some classics as well as some more recent books.

Take notes as you read. Highlight books you own. Tear out pages and place in folders to refer back to later when you start writing. Jot down ideas as books inspire your own thoughts. The books you read should inspire the content for your book. As you read, be sure to consider how you might make the book you write better than the ones you read.

In that same blog post, I offered eight more tips on how to research and write a book.

John Kremer's Advice to Would-Be Book Authors

1. Begin by reading a lot of books, especially on the subject you want to write about.

2. Sit down and start writing. Write one to four pages a day.

3. Outline your book.

4. Start at the beginning. Begin writing your book.

5. Research as you write.

6. Get feedback from someone you trust.

7. Don't give up.

8. Create content, no matter the format (book, audio, video, etc.).

9. Market your book as you write it.

BookMarketingBestsellers.com

34. Share interesting tidbits from your research.

You can share tips, facts, insights, and statistics you discovered as you did your research. Share things that didn't make it into your novel or book. Share the facts that became key items in your book.

In a post on Book Marketing Bestsellers, I shared the key insight I've learned in 30 years of marketing books. Read the entire *Making Friends: The Essence of Marketing* post here: https://bookmarketingbestsellers.com/the-essence-of-book-marketing-making-real-friends.

Here is a key insight I shared in that post:

When speaking to the Women Writers of the West conference several years ago, I realized that when I talked about creating relationships, I was really talking about making friends. Because that is what every good marketer really does: They make friends—real friends.

When you begin to think of marketing in this way, everything about marketing books becomes more fun. Suddenly there is no foreignness, no fear, no feelings of inadequacy.

We can all make friends. It's a talent we've had since we were little children. Use it.

Take time out today to make some new friends — not just acquaintances, but real friends. You can start with your social networks and eventually branch out to creating professional relationships that are made up of real friends.

Making Friends:
The Essence of Marketing

All of marketing ultimately comes down to one thing: **creating relationships**.

Here are four key tips to help you create effective business relationships:

1. Create your Kremer 100 list. Don't try to be friends with thousands or millions of people. You can't do it. Focus on 100 key media and marketing contacts.

2. Be persistent. Once you've developed a database of key contacts, you must be in touch with them on a regular basis — at least once a month. Tell them something new with each contact.

3. Create a word-of-mouth army. Since 80% of all books are sold by word-of-mouth, your primary goal in marketing your books is to create a core group of people who will spark that word-of-mouth.

4. Become a people person. If you are going to become a successful book promoter, you will have to cultivate a fun feeling when you go out into the public. If you genuinely care about people, you will have no problem facing the public. Just open your heart and let it out.

Source: http://bookmarketingbestsellers.com
/the-essence-of-book-marketing-making-real-friends

35. Review websites, blogs, books, courses, or events on writing.

You can write reviews of websites, blogs, courses, books, audios, videos, or events on writing, research, plotting, marketing, publicity, etc. Feature the logos or cover images in your blog post or article.

As a writer, sharing the resources you use in writing will be of interest to many readers of your blog. If you are not a writer but focused on another skill, you can write posts or articles on websites, etc. related to that skill.

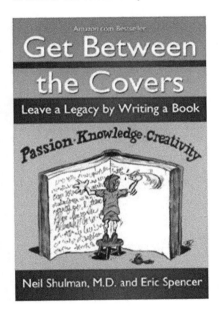

Here's a resource I shared during the week the authors were promoting an Amazon book launch for *Get Between the Covers* (https://openhorizons.blogspot.com/2006/12/get-between-covers.html):

Notice from a consulting client who has written a book you might be interested in:

*Dec. 28th Amazon.com Launch Date for **Get Between the Covers: Leave a Legacy by Writing a Book** by Neil Shulman, M.D. and Eric Spencer*

Mark your calendars! On Thursday, December 28, 2006, Get Between the Covers will have its official launch on Amazon.com with one goal in mind ... to get to #1 on the Bestseller List.

*We've put over 5 years of work into this book, which will hopefully lead tens of thousands, if not millions, to write a book in their lifetime and thus be able to share their knowledge, creativity, and experience with this generation as well as future ones. It's been endorsed by nearly all of the top people in the publishing industry—many of whom contributed material because of the influence they believe it will have. When people think about writing books, reading, or publishing, we want them to think **Get Between the Covers!***

*Why should you purchase **Get Between the Covers!** on the 28th?*

As part of purchasing this book on December 28th, you will be supporting several endeavors, including: a literary grant/scholarship program for both high school and college students that we are establishing which will encourage and enable them to write and publish books and a program that donates books to children who are less fortunate, so that they might develop a love for reading.

That's right, we will give ALL of the income received from book sales on the 28th to support these efforts! So, in addition to getting a copy of a book that you will enjoy if you have ideas for books and want to translate them to paper, or know a friend, family member, or co-worker who does, you will also be helping us to give back.

36. Share the novels or books you are reading now.

What's on your nightstand? What's in your purse or briefcase? What books did you take to the shore during vacation? You don't have to review these books. All you have to do is share them in a listing or discussion.

In a Facebook post, I shared some of the audiobooks my wife and I have enjoyed while driving between Taos and Southern California:

Some of my favorite books that my wife and I have listened to as audio books as we drove: Bel Canto, The Help, The Time Traveler's Wife, Eragon, and the mysteries of Tony Hillerman.

37. Survey your readers' opinions.

You can survey readers or website visitors on any key issue in your books or on your website. Surveys allows you to do several posts with essentially the same content:

Announce the survey.

Then promote the survey.

Then announce the results of the survey.

That will take at least three blog posts, probably more if you add updates over several weeks.

In the link below you can check out the results of a Self-Publishing Survey I conducted several years ago (https://bookmarketingbestsellers.com/self-publishing-survey-the-results).

What is your favorite platform for self-publishing?	
Amazon Kindle	33%
CreateSpace	33%
Ingram Spark	6%
BookBaby	0%
LuLu	3%
Smashwords	3%
Offset Book Printers	6%
Other	15%

38. Run a contest.

If you are a novelist, you can ask people to name their favorite character and describe why they like the character.

For nonfiction books, ask readers to describe the most important tip they learned from your book. Offer a free book, sample chapter from your new novel or book, a phone call from you, or something else as a prize.

For other products or services, run a contest related to your particular service or product. Or run a contest that targets the people you want to reach.

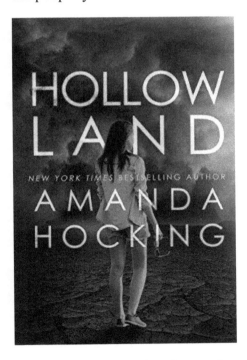

As part of her Zombiepalooza, Amanda Hocking ran a giveaway contest for her new novel *Hollowland*. Here are the details of her giveaway contest as outlined on her old blog at Blogspot.com (no longer active).

1. There will be three winners, with each person receiving one signed paperback of Hollowland.

2. The giveaway runs from today until midnight on Friday, October 31, 2011.

3. To enter: Comment below and with a way to contact you in case you win (email addresses work best).

4. Only one entry per person.

5. The winner will be chosen by Random.org.

39. Feature your reader comments in later blog posts or webpages.

If you get great reader comments, don't just let them sit in the comments section. Feature them in a blog post roundup of your favorite comments.

Recently I shared some of my favorite comments from an old website (Ask John Kremer) where I featured Q&A from readers: https://bookmarketingbestsellers.com/my-favorite-ask-john-kremer-comments.

Here is one of the comments:

Creating a product or service is easy. It's the marketing that's difficult, time-consuming and expensive. Put another way: It's easy to make a football. Getting it into the end zone is tough. – Denny Hatch, author of Career-Changing Takeaways

40. Encourage your readers to interview you.

Encourage your readers and social media followers to send in a series of questions you will answer.

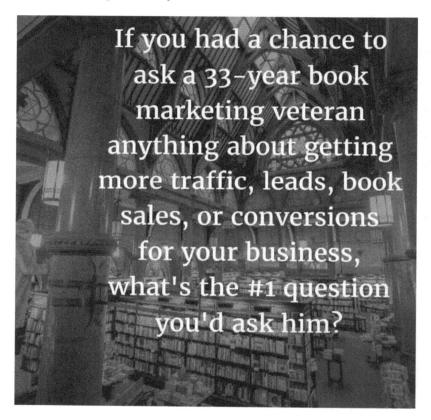

If you had a chance to ask a 33-year book marketing veteran anything about getting more traffic, leads, book sales, or conversions for your business, what's the #1 question you'd ask him?

In a Facebook post, I posed the following question: *If you had a chance to ask a 33-year book marketing veteran anything about getting more traffic, leads, book sales, or conversions for your business, what's the #1 question you'd ask him?*

As Facebook followers sent in questions via Facebook comments, I answered them. I then posted all the questions and answers in a post on Book Marketing Bestsellers: https://bookmarketingbestsellers.com/facebook-book-marketing-qa-good-stuff-here.

Here are two questions (and my answers) from that Facebook post:

Question: Are you "really published" if you pay a company to publish your book?

John Kremer: You are really published if your book is published as an ebook or a printed book, no matter how it comes about.

That said, your book probably won't sell many copies if you've paid the wrong company to publish your book. In most cases you are better off publishing your book yourself (see my cogent advice on your publishing options here: https://bookmarketingbestsellers.com/how-do-i-get-my-books-published) or getting a good mid-size publisher to fall in love with your book and marketing plan (and you!).

Question: Is it possible to get an industry star to review your book? What's the best way to do that and what if you don't have a connection to get you in?

John Kremer: It is possible to get an industry star or key influencer to review your book. Start by asking if you can interview them for your podcast (or video series or teleseminar).

Or find a friend who has interviewed them, or gotten a testimonial from them, or has featured them in their blog or social media somewhere.

Or, finally, go to a conference where the star is speaking. Ask her at the conference.

41. Write a pick-a-character post.

For novelists, ask your readers to pick which character in your novel is most like them. Then publish some of their choices in a blog post along with your comments.

For nonfiction authors, ask your readers to tell you which story you told most touched them.

Have you ever wanted to tell a fictional character to go to hell?

www.bookmarketingbestsellers.com

Or you could ask your readers questions like I asked in this post: https://bookmarketingbestsellers.com/talk-back-to-fictional-characters.

Have you ever wanted to tell a fictional character to go to hell?

Or just talk back to them?

Or warn them about the killer around the corner?

Or simply have a long conversation with them?

If so, which characters?

And what would you have said?

Please leave a comment below.

42. Reveal the character that is you.

If you write fiction, tell your readers which character in your novel is most like you.

For nonfiction authors, let them know which story has most meaning to you—and why.

For example, I would be the storyteller Thom Merrilin in *The World of Time* series by Robert Jordan. Check out the post I wrote featuring Thom's writing advice: https://bookmarketingbestsellers.com/writing-advice-from-the-wheel-of-time-series.

If you use the words people expect, they grow bored. A great ballad needs to be unexpected.

Never be expected.

When people start to expect you—when they start to anticipate your flourishes, to look for the ball you had hidden through sleight of hand, or to smile before you reached the twist line of your tale—it is time to pack up your cloak, bow once for good measure, and stroll away.

After all, that was what they'd least expect you to do when all was going well.

And here are a few of my comments:

Now, great fiction is always unexpected on some level or it doesn't make a great story.

But even nonfiction should be unexpected. If it's expected, it means that you are not revealing anything new. And if so, then why would they buy your book?

Writing Advice from The Wheel of Time

Here is some writing advice from Thom Merrilin, a storytelling character from *A Memory of Light*, book 14 of *The Wheel of Time* series . . .

If you use the words people expect, they grow bored.

A great ballad needs to be unexpected.

Never be expected.

When people start to expect you—when they start to anticipate your flourishes, to look for the ball you had hidden through sleight of hand, or to smile before you reached the twist line of your tale—it is time to pack up your cloak, bow once for good measure, and stroll away.

After all, that was what they'd least expect you to do when all was going well.

https://amzn.to/2N8AE3A

A MEMORY OF LIGHT

Robert Jordan
Brandon Sanderson

43. Interview book reviewers.

Pick some book reviewers, magazine editors, bloggers, TV producers, etc. who you want to create a relationship with. Then interview them on your blog, on your Internet radio show, via Facebook Live or Skype.

I've interviewed many newspaper editors, magazine editors, TV producers, and radio producers during live seminars.

During my People You Should Know teleseminar series, I interviewed Robyn Spizman, the *Today* show's gifting expert.

Here's a blog post I wrote on how to create relationships with key media people as Darrell Gurney did in 2008: https://bookmarketingbestsellers.com/interviews-how-to-create-relationships-with-key-media-people.

The post describes how Darrell created a relationship with a key syndicated columnist, Joyce Lain Kennedy, by first interviewing her for his teleseminar series.

44. Interview bloggers.

There are many opportunities to interview bloggers. You can, of course, always start with me.

Email: JohnKremer@BookMarket.com to set up an interview.

In the course of writing my many blogs, I've interviewed many bloggers and, in return, was interviewed by them.

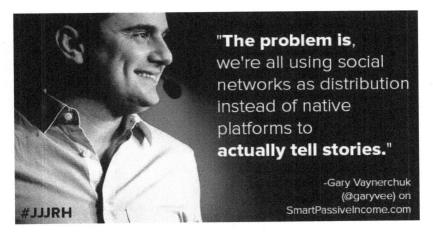

Pat Flynn of SmartPassiveIncome.com interviews top social media leaders as a way to build traffic to his website.

Here's a podcast where he interviews Gary Vaynerchuk, author of *Jab, Jab, Jab, Right Hook*, and CEO of Vayner Media: https://bookmarketingbestsellers.com/gary-vaynerchuk-how-to-win-with-social-media. Listen in for some great advice on using social media.

You can also use podcast interviews or Q&A text interviews to build your traffic. Be sure to interview people who have large audiences, high traffic websites, major podcasts, or lots of social media followers.

45. Interview booksellers.

Want to interview some booksellers? You can order a data
file list of the Top 900 Independent Bookstores by clicking
here: https://bookmarketingbestsellers.com/top-900-
independent-bookstores. This list of indie bookstores
features 950 top general interest bookstores. It includes
names of the book buyer and event coordinator, address,
phone, fax, email, website, Facebook and Twitter profiles,
and other details about each bookstore.

During my People You Should Know teleseminar series, I
interviewed Tim McCormick, senior buyer at Imagine
Nation Books and Books Are Fun (now known as
Collective Goods). Listen in to his interview here:
https://bookmarket.com/audios/Tim-McCormick.mp3.

46. Interview a celebrity in your field.

Interview experts and celebrities in your field of interest (the topic you specialize in). Celebrity and expert interviews are incredibly popular in almost every field.

In a video interview, Cameron Brain, co-founder of Xydo Curation, interviewed Michael Stelzner, founder of Social Media Examiner. Michael talked about SME's approach to content, what keeps visitors coming back, the tools they use to capture and grow their audience, and the future of content marketing.

Check out this very informative interview here: https://bookmarketingbestsellers.com/michael-stelzner-on-how-to-build-a-high-traffic-website.

47. Interview a major celebrity that has a passion for your field.

Look for celebrities who might not be experts in your topic, but who have a passion for the topic. For example, interview a movie star that loves dogs or is a vegetarian or fights for the preservation of the ocean. In this example, the celebrity should be passionate for the topic you write about.

Interview sports personalities, singers, movie stars, TV stars, social media celebrities, producers, editors, etc.

Here, for example, is an interview of a celebrity interior designer (excerpted from *Allure* magazine) on my old blog: https://openhorizons.blogspot.com/2011/04/books-add-warmth-to-any-room-miles-redd.html.

Miles Redd, an interior designer in New York City, loves books. As he noted in an interview in April's Allure Magazine: I love the look of books everywhere—in cases, on shelves, and in stacks on coffee and side tables. They give a room instant soul and warmth and show you have a curiosity about the world.

48. Feature your favorite bookstores.

Besides interviewing booksellers (as note in a point 45 above), you can also write about your favorite bookstores. Describe why you love them. Include photos.

I used to feature quotes from many independent bookstores on my old Ask the Booksellers blog. Here are a few excerpts from those blog posts:

Daniel Goldin of Boswell Book Company in Milwaukee, Wisconsin: *People buy anything that is hanging from the ceiling, even books.*

And a quote from Gibson's Bookstore: *If you like independent bookstores and what they do for you and what they represent, and you have one or more near you, buy books from them whenever you can. Narrow that gap.*

Or check out some of the great testimonials booksellers have sent to book authors as featured in one of my blog posts: https://bookmarketingbestsellers.com/bookseller-letters-you-would-love-to-get.

"Wow, this book keeps walking out the door. Kids really want to learn how to open all the doors to Hollywood!"

"I have read hundreds of self-help books over the years. I have admired the work of Wayne Dyer, Louise Hay, and Deepak Chopra, but Freedom to Love is now my Bible of inner transformation."

"We can't keep this book on the shelves during the holiday season. People often buy multiple copies for their friends."

"If you have customers who care about what happens in the Third World, they'll love this book."

"My regular customers who are therapists love this book. They often buy multiple copies."

"We keep a copy of Laughter: The Drug of Choice in the back room for when we need a break. It's great fun!"

Your job: Get testimonials like this from some of your favorite indie booksellers. It's not hard to get these blurbs if you work with your independent bookstores to sell copies of your books. The ask for the testimonial.

Yes, you have to ask for the testimonial. I have rarely found booksellers who will volunteer blurbs even when they like you. You have to ask.

49. Interview your favorite book authors.

Interview your favorite book authors, whether related to your topic or not. Track them down at conferences and ask them if they'd do a quick Facebook Live interview with you. Or track them down through friends to ask for the interview.

The best interviews, obviously, would be with famous authors who have large fan bases that would track down the author's interview on your website.

You can again check out the wonderful Skype interview I did with Bevan Atkinson, author of *The Tarot Mysteries* series. Learn how an accidental detective uses her intuition, inspired by the Tarot, to solve murders! And learn how an author listens to her characters as she writes! https://bookmarketingbestsellers.com/bevan-atkinson-how-to-listen-to-voices-when-writing.

50. Write a poem.

Or write a limerick. Or share a short story. Or share a song (one that you wrote and performed, or one of your favorite songs from a celebrity singer).

I shared the following prose poem when I discovered my poem had been featured in a Yahoo Answers question: https://bookmarketingbestsellers.com/waterfall-a-prose-poem-by-john-kremer.

Which poem utilizes the poetic devices of imagery and rhythm?

A) John Kremer's "Waterfall"
B) Emily Dickinson's "Heart! We will forget him!"
C) Robert Frost's "The Road Not Taken"
D) Aleksandr Solzhenitsyn's "A Storm in the Mountains"

Check it out: My poem was mentioned in the same breath as poems by Emily Dickinson, Robert Frost, and Aleksandr Solzhenitsyn. That's incredible company to be in. Here's my poem that was featured in the above question:

Waterfall a prose poem by John Kremer

I found the strangest waterfall in a narrow channel along a flat plain in the gully near my home. It was too flat for a fall, and yet I heard the unmistakable gurgle of a waterfall. So I crawled down into the belly of the gully to check it out more closely.

Even at close range, the water still appeared to run across a plain without a fall. But then I saw what looked like a hole in the middle of the flowing stream. So I picked up a stick to poke around to check how deep it was. Well, in doing so, I upset the hole and the gurgle and everything.

Whatever hole might have been there I blocked, then plugged up, then eliminated altogether. Whatever fall might have been there, I leveled. Whatever channel might have been there, I eroded. I ended up with a flat alluvial plain, flowing smoothly, making no soothing gurgle, and loaded with mud, mud, mud.

The whole thing was just a result of the uncertainty principle, which simply says that you can't have your cake and eat it too.

The moment you touch something, you change it irreversibly, and forever. Any contact of any kind with anything results in change — change both in the thing and in you. You're never the same again. You can't be. And neither can it.

But that's the beauty as well as the horror. It's frightening sometimes to think of the power we have to change each other, to change a small part of the world. But that's the beauty as well. That opportunity to create an entire new world through every small change we make — that opportunity is glorious, and one I'd never pass up, not for all the undecaying gold in the world.

I destroyed that waterfall today and, in so doing, I lost something. But I gained something, too. I gained contact. I touched, and though I somehow destroyed by that touch, I also created — something perhaps no better, maybe worse, but something that now carries a part of me forever.

That's always something more.

And that something more is precious.

Waterfall

Prose poem by John Kremer

I found the strangest waterfall in a narrow channel along a flat plain in the gully near my home. It was too flat for a fall, and yet I heard the unmistakable gurgle of a waterfall. So I crawled down into the belly of the gully to check it out more closely.

Even at close range, the water still appeared to run across a plain without a fall. But then I saw what looked like a hole in the middle of the flowing stream. So I picked up a stick to poke around to check how deep it was.

Well, in doing so, I upset the hole and the gurgle and everything. Whatever hole might have been there I blocked, then plugged up, then eliminated altogether. Whatever fall might have been there, I leveled. Whatever channel might have been there, I eroded. I ended up with a flat alluvial plain, flowing smoothly, making no soothing gurgle, and loaded with mud, mud, mud.

The whole thing was just a result of the uncertainty principle, which simply says that you can't have your cake and eat it too.

The moment you touch something, you change it irreversibly, and forever. Any contact of any kind with anything results in change — change both in the thing and in you. You're never the same again. You can't be. And neither can it.

But that's the beauty as well as the horror. It's frightening sometimes to think of the power we have to change each other, to change a small part of the world. But that's the beauty as well. That opportunity to create an entire new world through every small change we make — that opportunity is glorious, and one I'd never pass up, not for all the undecaying gold in the world.

I destroyed that waterfall today and, in so doing, I lost something. But I gained something, too. I gained contact. I touched, and though I somehow destroyed by that touch, I also created — something perhaps no better, maybe worse, but something that now carries a part of me forever.

That's always something more.

And that something more is precious.

51. Expose your inner being.

Share your feelings. Let people see something that you are really passionate about, something you really care about. It's okay once in awhile to open up your heart, your mind, or your soul to others.

Miracles: You do not have to look for them. They are there, 24/7, beaming like radio waves all around you. Put up the antenna, turn up the volume — snap... crackle... this just in, every person you talk to is a chance to change the world. — **Hugh Elliott**

https://bookmarketingbestsellers.com/book-marketing-tip-how-to-change-the-world

Here's something I shared on Book Marketing Bestsellers, including a great quote and my comment on that quote: https://bookmarketingbestsellers.com/book-marketing-tip-how-to-change-the-world.

Here's a great quote from Hugh Elliott, former blogger at Standing Room Only:

Miracles: You do not have to look for them. They are there, 24/7, beaming like radio waves all around you. Put up the antenna, turn up the volume - snap... crackle... this just in, every person you talk to is a chance to change the world. — Hugh Elliott, blogger, Standing Room Only

Remember that when you need to make that one more phone call, or write that one more email, or make one more effort to send out a news release or book proposal. Every person you talk to is a chance to change the world. What are you waiting for?

I loved that quote from Hugh. I really resonate with it. Miracles: Every person you talk to is a chance to change the world.

52. Let people know about your day.

As with many social media users, I've share things about my day in a good number of tweets:

Going out now to walk with my wife and two dogs. Beautiful day for it. Will walk 3 miles.

Had 3 inches of snow on Friday nite. Lost power for 12 hrs. Phone is offline as well. Power good now. Phone to be fixed Monday. Life in Taos.

I also shared personal info and photos on Facebook:

A photo of me and my dog Becky near our home outside of Taos, New Mexico. Taken a little over a year or so ago. Whoops, it's been a little over three years ago. Just confirmed.

53. Post photos of your favorite book authors.

You can post photos or videos of your favorite book authors, novelists, or poets. Be sure to write a warm personal introduction to the photos or videos.

In a post on my old Book Marketing Bestsellers blog (https://openhorizons.blogspot.com/2007/12/wow-what-photographs-what-video.html), I shared several photos and a video from photography Gregory Colbert, author of several books.

The photos are incredible. So is the video. Make sure you watch it at the link above.

Gregory Colbert has used both still and movie cameras to explore extraordinary interactions between humans and animals. His exhibition, Ashes and Snow, consists of over 50 large-scale photographic artworks, a 60-minute film, and two 9-minute film haikus.

Thanks to Kira Rosner for sharing these with me. And now I share them with you. Enjoy your new year.

54. Join in Amazon Bestseller Campaigns.

Join in the promotional campaigns of your favorite fellow authors, mundane as well as famous. Promote these campaigns via your blog. You can join Amazon bestseller campaigns, book giveaways, launch parties, telesummits, product launches, and other promotional campaigns for books or authors.

In a post on my Book Marketing Bestsellers blog (https://openhorizons.blogspot.com/2006/04/daughter-of-yellow-river-amazon.html), I encouraged other authors to participate in Diana Lu's Amazon campaign for *Daughter of the Yellow River*.

Here's an excerpt from my post:

If you ever thought of doing your own Amazon.com bestseller campaign, then you might want to check into the campaign now being done for Diane Lu's Daughter of the

Yellow River. Why? Because she has so many participants, including people mailing to their lists as well as dozens and dozens giving away free reports, audios, etc. to buyers of her book. Her list of movers and givers could be contacted to help you as well, especially if your book is on relationships, health, self-help, business, motivation, or related topics.

I don't generally participate in these Amazon.com bestseller campaigns. I think they've been overdone, but I do know their power in getting attention for your book online. So I still encourage authors to do a campaign at least once in the life of their book, no matter how new or old the book is.

55. Join in blog tours.

Blog tours were one of the hot ways to launch a book about 15 years ago. There are still reasons to do a blog tour and if a fellow book author does one, you can join their tour by hosting a Facebook Live, a Q&A on your website, a guest blog post, etc. And then you can also promote these blog tours via your blog.

When Stella Togo was doing a blog tour for her book, *The Million Dollar Seed*, she wrote a guest post for Book Marketing Bestsellers on how to write a blog post: https://bookmarketingbestsellers.com/stella-togo-the-5-minute-guide-to-writing-a-blog-post.

Besides providing some tips on how to write great blog posts, it also established her credibility as an expert. Plus, it provided my website with some great content!

56. Have a reader interview one of your characters with you responding as the character.

This above tip is for novelists. For nonfiction authors, have readers send in a list of questions for an expert to answer. Ask the expert to respond via your blog.

Here is an example of a book blogger (The Book Buff) interviewing a character in a novel, *Dracula in Love* by Karen Essex. Mina Harker talks about Count Dracula: https://thebookbuff.blogspot.com/2011/07/interview-with-mina-harker.html. Below is part of that interview.

Q: Ms. Harker, journalists and vampire hunters have been trying to track you down for one hundred thirteen years. Why did you choose now to come out with your own—and, may I say, startlingly different—version of the story?

Ms. Harker: As you can imagine, I needed to wait until some people died, and in my circle, death can take a very long time, if it comes at all. Also, for a long time, I thought my story too outlandish for the public to accept. I did not wish to be scorned as a fantasist or attention seeker. But whereas humans once shuddered at the very notion vampires, now more and more "normal" humans are fantasizing about becoming one. The timing seemed perfect.

Besides, this is the age of the tell-all, so I am telling all; I'm just omitting the modern habit of going into rehab first. I find this need to repent for, be cured of, and then confess one's "transgressions," a tedious aspect of today's culture. I prefer to keep a stiff Victorian upper lip. I am telling my story; I am not confessing it. Do you know the expression, "never complain, never explain?" My version is "never repent, never recant."

Q: Well, I confess that I found some of your revelations surprising and shocking. Without revealing any spoilers, you take us on a journey that crosses centuries and introduces exotic mythological creatures into what used to be a traditional vampire tale. Are we really to believe this hidden history of blood-drinking?

Ms. Harker: Modern readers have no idea of the real roots of the vampire. Bram Stoker gathered a lot of information, some of it true and some of it based on old wives' tales. He simplified a very complicated matter for easier public consumption, creating rules for the vampire's creation and destruction. Please! As I say in the book, crosses and garlic have no power in the supernatural world!

People love things served up in the form of good versus evil, though we all know that reality is always more complex. There have always been sexy, scary blood-drinkers, and there have always been immortals— obviously. I'm not going to explain it to you again. You did read the book, didn't you?

57. Report about promotions of others.

You can write about the promotional activities, launch parties, and other activities that your fellow book authors or internet marketers do. Comment as well on what they are doing. Writing about others is a great way to begin a relationship with other authors.

On my website, I showcased the book release party invitation for Donald Calvanese's fantasy novel *Carcium: The Conflict Begins*. https://bookmarketingbestsellers.com/sample-invitation-to-a-book-release-party.

Notice all the local celebrities who will attend the party. That's a great way to get the town talking about your book.

A Personal Invitation From Author & Fantasy Fiction Novelist Donald Calvanese

Agawam Mayor Richard A. Cohen
Agawam Town Clerk Richard M. Theroux
Agawam School Superintendent William P. Sapelli
Attorney John Tatoian • DonQ Rum • Don Sebastiani & Sons
Martignetti Companies • M.S. Walker, Inc. • Saint Mary's Academy
Tate Publishing • The Eastern States Exposition
West Springfield Mayor Edward Gibson
West Springfield Lions Past President Don Del Bouno

Cordially Invite You & Your Guests
To The National Book Release Celebration Of

"Carcium — The Conflict Begins"
A Fantasy Fiction Novel By Author Donald Calvanese

Wednesday, November 2, 2011
6 to 10 p.m.
Storrowton Tavern & Carriage House, 1305
Memorial Avenue,
West Springfield, Massachusetts

Featured Speakers:
Mayor Richard A. Cohen
Andy Calvanese, Jr.
Donald Calvanese
Don Del Bouno
Wayne McCary
& Several Surprise Guests

Complementary Hors d'oeuvres & Drinks Served.
Business Casual Attire Requested.

This event will benefit the library at Saint Mary's
Academy in Longmeadow. A portion of book sales
will be donated to the school.

RSVP requested only by emailing
rsvp@carcium.com. Contact Michele at
413.262.4224 or michele@carcium.com for
additional information.

For more information about Author Donald
Calvanese, the Carcium book series and to
purchase the book online, visit www.carcium.com.

58. Ask readers to vote.

Have readers vote for variations of your book covers, book titles, advertising copy, news releases,

In 1997, I asked my website visitors to select between two versions of the cover for the 5th edition of my *1001 Ways to Market Your Books*. Cover A was selected by a margin of 9 to 1 over Cover B. Over 200 website visitors voted. Check out the two covers below:

Cover A   **Cover B**

You, too, can test your covers in this way. While you can't tell a book by its cover, you can sell a book by its cover. Hence, cover design is crucial to the success of your book. Be sure to test your covers. Use your website and social media to help you conduct tests.

59. Write guest posts on other blogs.

Writing guest posts is a great way to exchange blog posts with other authors. Plus, of course, it exposes you, your book, and your blog to other readers.

I've done many guest posts. They aren't hard to arrange. Find a great blogger who you are friends with or who is influential in your field. Then ask. Yes, you might have to ask more than once.

The Book Marketing Network
For book/ebook authors, publishers, & self-publishers

Another way to find bloggers who might be interested in a guest post from you is to join The Book Marketing Network (https://www.thebookmarketingnetwork.com), where you can hook up with other book authors to guest post on each other's blog.

Jeff Davidson, author of *Breathing Space*, has written a number of guest posts for my website. Here are a few of the links featuring his posts:

Jeff Davidson: Make the Most of Your Speeches: https://bookmarketingbestsellers.com/jeff-davidson-make-the-most-of-your-speeches

Jeff Davidson: Tools in Your Book Author Arsenal: https://bookmarketingbestsellers.com/jeff-davidson-tools-in-your-book-author-arsenal

Jeff Davidson: Author Interview Questions: https://bookmarketingbestsellers.com/jeff-davidson-author-interview-questions

Jeff Davidson: Grappling with Your To-Do List:
https://bookmarketingbestsellers.com/jeff-davidson-grappling-with-your-to-do-list

Jeff Davidson: 10 Tips for Becoming a Successful Mainstream Author:
https://bookmarketingbestsellers.com/jeff-davidson-10-tips-for-becoming-a-successful-mainstream-author

Jeff Davidson: Choosing an Article Topic:
https://bookmarketingbestsellers.com/jeff-davidson-choosing-an-article-topic

Jeff Davidson: Choosing an Article Topic:
https://bookmarketingbestsellers.com/jeff-davidson-choosing-an-article-topic

60. Post photos of your fans.

Post photos of your fans. Feature them reading your book. Or use your smartphone to take a photo of people who buy your book direct from you.

Several years ago, I saw a book trailer video where three fans were reading their friend's comic novel and laughing away. It was a great trailer that any author could duplicate with the help of a few friends. Check out the video here: https://bookmarketingbestsellers.com/fun-viral-book-trailer-incredibly-easy-to-duplicate-for-any-book.

Many blogging platforms allow you to showcase people who follow or fan your blog. Blogger.com and WordPress both have this capability as do social networks like Facebook, Twitter, and LinkedIn.

David Park, author of *The More You Do The Better You Feel*, has taken over 1,000 photos of people who have bought his book. Check out a few of the photos here: https://davidparkerauthor.com/resources/reader-photos.

61. Ask readers to send photos.

Run a promotion asking readers to send you photos of them reading your book in unusual places: foreign locations, mountaintops, in the water, at the dining room table, in a restaurant, while standing in line for the latest version of the iPhone, while dancing a jig, at a location featured in your novel or book, up a tree, down a sewer, at the zoo (perhaps with a monkey reading your book), in a bookstore.

There is a hashtag on Instagram for people to share books. #bookstagram is *an Instagram hashtag used to denote a book-related picture. It can be an image of someone reading the book, the book itself, or objects that evoke something (plot, characters, themes) from the book. Images can be of the reader's favorite reading spot at home, a shot of taking the book on an adventure or vacation, or a favorite local coffee shop or bookstore.*

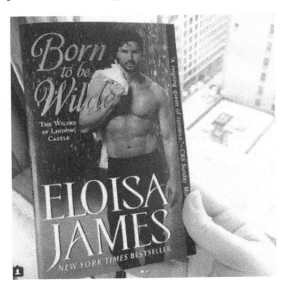

Many magazines encourage their readers to send in photos of them reading the magazine in exotic locales.

62. Feature photos of yourself with your book in different locations.

Have fun with it. Make it a game for yourself. See how many different locations you can visit to take a photo of yourself holding your book.

Mandy Lender blogged about being the first author to sign a book in four U.S. states at the same moment in time. He shared the above photo on his Facebook page.

I created a **Book Marketing Photo Wall** featuring book authors holding their books. Among the authors are Kareem Abdul-Jabbar, John Kremer, and Mary Watson. You can still submit your photo this wall. Details here: https://bookmarketingbestsellers.com/book-marketing-photos-book-authors-holding-their-books.

63. Feature social media posts where others write about you or your book.

With Twitter, it's easy to retweet anyone who mentions you or your book. You can do the same with Facebook, Pinterest, or LinkedIn. Of course, you can also blog about your tweets and Facebook posts.

Here's a Facebook comment on one of my recent Facebook posts:

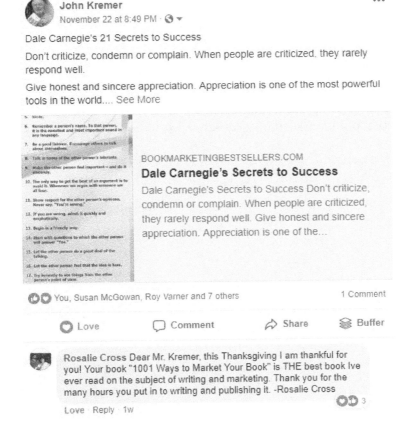

Dear Mr. Kremer, this Thanksgiving I am thankful for you! Your book "1001 Ways to Market Your Book" is THE best book I've ever read on the subject of writing and marketing. Thank you for the many hours you put in to writing and publishing it. - Rosalie Cross

And here's another Facebook comment on one of my Facebook posts:

Charles Betterton – Words of wisdom from John Kremer, THE book marketing expert who has helped sell over a billion books already and is working on the next billion, perhaps including YOURS!

Tweets

And here are a few tweets I retweeted because they mentioned me:

@abeasl123 You need @JohnKremer He's the man when it comes to book marketing ideas https://bookmarketingbestsellers.com

@BrynaKranzler 36 Ways to Help a Book Author You Love http://bit.ly/bRfDrC Thank you, @JohnKremer

64. Create a controversy.

Comment on a news story, blog post, current event, historical event, website, or tweet. Say something outrageous and let 'er rip.

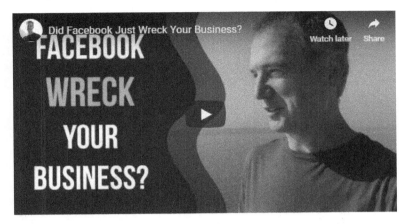

Jeff Walker, the Product Launch King, produced a video asking a key question when Facebook changed its algorithm for displaying Facebook posts: Did Facebook Just Wreck Your Business? Check out Jeff's video here: https://bookmarketingbestsellers.com/facebook-has-made-some-big-changes-will-they-affect-you.

Here are three big takeaways from Jeff's video.

Discover the #1 way to protect yourself from future algorithm changes on any social media networks.

Discover the only platform over the past 22 years that has always produced great results.

Discover a simple strategy that crushes free social media tactics (and helps you build a real, profitable business).

65. Write about a service you used.

For authors, write about a service you used in writing or promoting your book. If you like, tell your followers why you liked or did not like the service.

 John Kremer @JohnKremer · Nov 16
A great video service for authors: Is your book or novel a great book? - bookmarketingbestsellers.com/great-books-ar...

Here are a few of the tweets I've shared during the past year where I showcase services and resources useful to writers:

TwitCount - A Free Fix for the Broken Twitter Share Counts http://twitcount.com via @twitcountapp

10 Comic Blogs That Every Comic Book Fan Should Read - https://www.makeuseof.com/tag/10-comic-blogs-comic-book-fan-read

In today's world, if I were to do only one thing to market my books, it would be to use Derek Doepker's Automatic Book Sales System. Check it out here: https://ebookbestsellersecrets.com/automaticreplayjohn. The replay is good for four days only.

Free business and marketing ebooks to read at
http://freebooksforall.com/business.htm

Facebook Posts

Book Title Critique Service by John Kremer - Create a
brandable memorable bestselling book title! With a special
Nanowrimo discount! -
https://bookmarketingbestsellers.com/book-title-critiques

Publish Authority
November 15 at 2:46 PM · 🌐

👍 **Like Page** ···

#Authors, Also market your book (and self) via podcasting. Here's a trove of
podcasting directories and tools via John Kremer >
http://bookmarketingbestsellers.com/podcasting-tools/

#podcasts #amwriting #booksbooksbooks #ThursdayThought
#hybridpublishing

And a Facebook post from Charles Betterton:

*If you are interested in ANY aspect of writing, publishing,
or marketing you might want to attend Judith Briles' 8th
Annual Author Youniversity Extravaganza in Breckenridge,
Colorado August 23-26!*

66. Share a quote you like.

I love quotes, so I share a lot of them on all my blogs.

Here's a quote I shared on my Book Marketing Bestsellers website: https://bookmarketingbestsellers.com/antoine-de-saint-exupery-on-building-a-ship.

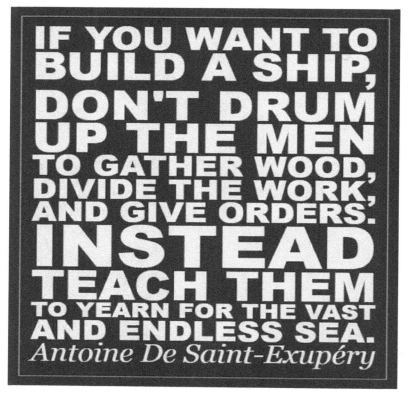

If you want to build a ship, don't drum up the men to gather the wood, divide the work, and give orders. Instead, teach them to yearn for the vast and endless sea. — Antoine de Saint-Exupéry

And here's my book marketing comment on that quote:

And, if you want to sell books, don't drum up humdrum followers. Teach your fans to yearn for what your book offers. Teach them to yearn for your knowledge, your experience, your entertainment, your passion.

Teach them to yearn for their own passion. Show them that your book fulfills that passion.

You can find many other quotes related to book marketing here: https://bookmarketingbestsellers.com/book-marketing-quotes.

And here are many quotes providing inspiration for book readers: https://bookmarketingbestsellers.com/inspiration-for-book-readers.

67. Share your social media posts.

Instead of keeping your social media posts isolated on Facebook or Twitter or LinkedIn or Pinterest, you can reshare your best social media shares on your website or via your email newsletter.

John Kremer ✓
@JohnKremer

Book marketing is what I do. I teach people how to market their ebooks/books, both online and off. Promote your books: bookmarketingbestsellers.com

⊚ Taos, New Mexico

🔗 bookmarket.com

Here's one post I wrote to share some tweets I had made that week: https://bookmarketingbestsellers.com/book-marketing-tweets-for-may-2014.

More powerful than the New York Times: A single-author blog with a passionate following.
https://bookmarketingbestsellers.com/the-power-of-single-author-blogs

If you write four pages a day, you'll have a book in less than six months. #books #authors
https://bookmarketingbestsellers.com/john-kremers-advice-to-would-be-book-authors

Is your book dangerous? Will it change people's lives? If not, keep writing and revising.
https://bookmarketingbestsellers.com/helen-exley-books-can-change-your-life

If you tell a good story, people will hang on your words. — David Attenborough #words #stories
https://bookmarketingbestsellers.com/david-attenborough-on-the-art-of-storytelling

Here's how you attract attention and sell more books: Tell Good Stories! #books #stories
https://bookmarketingbestsellers.com/david-attenborough-on-the-art-of-storytelling

As a writer, you get to play, you get to alter time, you get to come up with smart lines. #writers –
https://bookmarketingbestsellers.com/iain-banks-on-being-a-writer

Steps to Becoming a Happier Person: Read more books. Read many more books.
https://bookmarketingbestsellers.com/5-steps-to-becoming-a-happier-person ... #books #authors #reading

68. Write a how-to post.

For novelists, tell people how to cook a dish featured in your novel, or how to sew a corset, or how to sail the seven seas, or how to spot a vampire. Be sure that your how-to post relates to your novel.

For nonfiction authors, feature tips or how-to advice related to your book.

Several years ago, I wrote a blog post to feature 14 reasons an author should be active on Pinterest: https://bookmarketingbestsellers.com/7-reasons-you-should-be-active-on-pinterest.

The original 7 reasons, over time, became 14 reasons why any book author should be on Pinterest.

No matter what kind of book you have written or product you have created or service you offer, Pinterest can send you a ton of avid customers to your website, sales page, email squeeze page, Amazon book page, Clickbank product link, Facebook page, etc.

> Pinterest is a key search engine. Over 2 billion searches are made on Pinterest every month
>
> CLICK TO TWEET 🐦

> The average order value of sales coming from Pinterest is $50 (Shopify) #Pinterest
>
> CLICK TO TWEET 🐦

> 80% of pins are repins. Repins are what makes Pinterest incredibly viral. #Pinterest
>
> CLICK TO TWEET 🐦

69. Create videos.

Create short engaging videos about you, your book, or your topic. Then post them to YouTube and embed them in a blog post on your website. Also post them to Facebook, Twitter, LinkedIn, Pinterest, etc.

Check out this video I created on advertisements in ebooks: https://openhorizons.blogspot.com/2011/04/ebook-advertisments-video-reveals-7.html.

There are so many ways to make videos now, including Facebook Live, Skype videos, YouTube videos, and so many low-cost video making programs.

70. Share any video that inspires you.

You can even share videos that are off-topic, videos that you simply love.

A recent post for My Incredible Website featured an up-and-coming viral video that showcases beautiful locations around the world and some wonderful dance moves: http://www.myincrediblewebsite.com/dance-like-no-one-is-watching.

This viral music/dance video features beautiful locations around the world! - The above video should have gone mega viral. For some reason it didn't, but you'll still love this video. It will inspire you.

Great song, wonderful dancing, exotic locations, incredible editing. Check it out. You'll be glad you did.

71. Create a video channel playlist.

Create a video playlist, and then embed it on your blog. YouTube allows you to make a playlist in just a few minutes.

Your video playlist, of course, should be focused on your keyword topic. For example, romance or romance novels, business management, gardening tips, cookie recipes, etc. Own your topic, and make sure your playlist has a name incorporating your keywords.

Check out my Book Marketing Tips Playlist on YouTube: https://www.youtube.com/playlist?list=PLBmBDUpR8MY JccMHTCuq-loHZ5ORYPso3.

And here is the playlist embedded in a blog post on my website: https://bookmarketingbestsellers.com/book-marketing-tips-video-playlist.

72. Share a song you really like.

Link to a music video on YouTube or to a song on a music site where people can buy the song.

Minutes after Susan Boyle's original video from Britain's Got Talent TV show went viral on YouTube (https://www.youtube.com/watch?v=wnn6mShs1P8), I shared a link because I found her singing and story so inspirational. I tweeted about it. I posted it on Facebook. And I blogged about it.

I love the ending of Beethoven's 9th Symphony, especially the *Ode to Joy*. And this flash mob performance of the *Ode to Joy* is itself full of joy. Fantastico!

Here are four flash mob performances of the final movement of Beethoven's 9th Symphony: http://www.myincrediblewebsite.com/ode-to-joy-flash-mob-performances. Amazing what he composed when he was nearly deaf.

73. Share a photo you really like.

You can share photos you love, especially photos related to your main topic.

Something like this wonderful library desk made of books that I featured on my Book Marketing Bestsellers blog: https://openhorizons.blogspot.com/2010/09/cool-library-desk-created-completely.html.

And here's a photo I shared that was taken by a good friend of mine: http://www.myincrediblewebsite.com/a-beautiful-mountain-scene.

74. Feature a magazine excerpt.

When you read a magazine article that you like, feature an excerpt from that article. Again, it's best to feature articles related to the topic of your book.

One of my hobby activities is developing a book on weight loss tips. Here's a recipe for Be Sassy Water excerpted from an article in *Prevention* magazine that might make it into my new book: http://celebrityweightlosstips.com/be-sassy-water.

Here is a healthy substitute for the sodas, diet drinks, coffee, and teas you have been drinking.

8 cups water
1 tsp ginger, freshly grated
1 medium cucumber, peeled & sliced thin
1 medium lemon, sliced thin
12 mint leaves

Mix all ingredients together in a large pitcher. Let the flavors blend overnight in your refrigerator.

The next morning, strain the water to eliminate the bulky stuff.

Drink this Be Sassy drink throughout the day.

You should finish the pitcher by the end of the day.

If you work outside the home, bring your water along in a good container.

Source: https://www.prevention.com/flat-belly-diet-meals-chart-and-sassy-water-recipe.

Be Sassy Water for Life & Health

Here is a really healthy substitute for the sodas, diet drinks, coffee, and teas you have been drinking.

8 cups water

1 tsp ginger, freshly grated

1 medium cucumber, peeled & sliced thin

1 medium lemon, sliced thin

12 mint leaves

Mix all ingredients together in a large pitcher. Let the flavors blend overnight in your refrigerator. The next morning, strain the water to eliminate the bulky stuff.

Drink this Be Sassy drink throughout the day. You should finish the pitcher by the end of the day.

If you work outside the home, bring your water along in a good container.

Source: http://www.prevention.com/flat-belly -diet-meals-chart-and-sassy-water-recipe

75. Offer a freebie for download.

To encourage people to follow your blog, sign up for your newsletter, or buy a new product from you, start by offering them a free ebook, free video, free audio, free chart, free poll results, free report, free white paper, etc.

A number of years ago, I offered a collection of my quotations as an ebook, *The Quotable John Kremer*, to entice readers to sign up for the teleseminars I was doing: https://openhorizons.blogspot.com/2011/04/quotations-from-john-kremer-get-book.html. Here is an image from the book:

Every book deserves
at least three years
of attention from the writer,
even if that involves
only a few minutes each day.
The constant, everyday attention
on marketing your book
works more wonders
than all the money you could throw
at all the marketing options
paraded before authors every day.

John Kremer, BookMarketingBestsellers.com

Here are a few of the quotations I shared in the blog post:

All of business ultimately comes down to one thing: creating relationships. If you don't understand this basic principle, you will ultimately fail as a business person.

Ask. That's where the magic and the power is—in doing that which you know you need to do. No matter what the obstacles. No matter what your trepidation. No matter how impossible it might seem. Nothing happens unless you do it. No media or market can respond to you until you ask for a response. No sales, no TV interviews, no major reviews, nothing—until you ask. Ask today.

Bookstores don't buy books (they simply rent them). It's readers who buy books. So ask the real buyers to buy your book. Promote to them.

Don't sell yourself short. No one will value you. Set a fair price for you, your book, your services, whatever it is that you have to offer. Most of us set way too low a price. Put it a little higher than you would normally be inclined to do. The worst that can happen is someone will come along and steal it.

If something really needs to be done and you don't enjoy doing it, find someone else who does enjoy doing that and hire them.

Love is the driving force for all marketing. Or it should be. Without love, it's all just politics, not business.

If you want to sell more books, there is one basic principle that is essential: Do something every day for every book you love. Call someone. Write a letter. Create Internet links. Update your web site. Write a related blog. Give a talk. Dance a jig.

76. Cross-pollinate.

If you have more than one blog, feature blog posts from your other blogs.

Besides my Book Marketing Bestsellers blog, I also blog at MyIncredibleWebsite.com, CelebrityWeightLossTips.com, and InfographicADay.com.

I often share posts from my other blogs or, at the very least, write a short post pointing to the full post on one of my other blogs.

For example, I excerpted five key writing tips for book authors from Blake Bailey, author of *Farther & Wilder: The Lost Weekends and Literary Dreams of Charles Jackson* from http://infographicaday.com/blake-bailey-bookographic-5-writing-tips and posted to my website at https://bookmarketingbestsellers.com/blake-bailey-5-writing-tips-for-book-authors.

This content was actually more appropriate for my book marketing site, even though it was also appropriate for my InfographicADay.com website.

1. Write about things that really interest you. Pick a subject that bores you and you'll write a boring book.

2. Be quiet and listen. Let the person talk.

3. Action is character. Let us see and hear how your characters behave.

4. Be prepared. Do your research. Find your structure. Then write.

5. If possible, be funny.

5 Writing Tips

by Blake Bailey

1. **Write about things that really interest you.**

   Pick a subject that bores you and you'll write a boring book.

2. **Be quiet and listen.**

   Let the person talk.

3. **Action is character.**

   Let us see and hear how your characters behave.

4. **Be prepared.**

   Do your research. Find your structure. Then write.

5. **If possible, be funny.**

FARTHER & WILDER

The Lost Weekends and Literary Dreams of Charles Jackson

BLAKE BAILEY

AUTHOR OF CHEEVER, WINNER OF THE NATIONAL BOOK CRITICS CIRCLE AWARD

http://amzn.to/2D8yrfF

77. Index your blog.

If your website is powered by WordPress, you can automatically index your blog via the categories and tags you assign to each post.

But I also index my blog by topics. Here, for example, are the book marketing index pages for my Book Marketing Bestsellers website (under the Book Marketing tab at the top of each page on the website).

https://bookmarketingbestsellers.com/book-marketing-articles-and-tips

https://bookmarketingbestsellers.com/book-marketing-how-to-market-novels-and-poetry

https://bookmarketingbestsellers.com/book-launches-and-product-launches

https://bookmarketingbestsellers.com/book-marketing-inspiration

https://bookmarketingbestsellers.com/book-marketing-freebies

https://bookmarketingbestsellers.com/book-marketing-gifs

https://bookmarketingbestsellers.com/book-marketing-quotes

I also include other index pages under the other major tabs on my website: Publicity, Internet Marketing, Publishing, Ebooks (and self-publishing), Authors, and Podcast & A/V.

78. Share content from a book.

For example, here are some great first line from bestselling novels: https://bookmarketingbestsellers.com/first-lines-in-books-draw-the-reader-in-make-them-great.

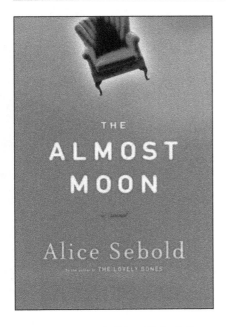

In a review of Alice Sebold's new novel The Almost Moon, the reviewer quoted the first lines of her new novel and then quoted the first lines from her previous novel, The Lovely Bones, as well.

In her first novel, The Lovely Bones, it took Alice two lines to kill off the heroine:

"My name was Salmon, like the fish; first name, Susie. I was fourteen when I was murdered on December 6, 1973."
— The Lovely Bones

What great first lines! They draw you into the novel right away. Lots of little details that flash!

In her newest novel The Almost Moon, Sebold gets to murder within the very first line:

"When all is said and done, killing my mother came easily."

Another great first line. It juxtaposes a cliche (when all is said and done) with a simple statement of murder. Incredibly dramatic in an understated way.

Would you continue reading if you had read these opening lines?

How does your book (fiction or nonfiction) stack up in drawing readers into your book?

And here's the first line from Jennifer Egan's novel, A Visit from the Goon Squad:

"It began the usual way, in the bathroom of the Lassimo Hotel."

Quiet, interesting, intriguing. Would you keep reading?

79. Share a great line from a TV show or movie.

Share a great line or a great image from a TV show or move. The TV show or movie should be current and hot, a classic, or right on target for your topic. Or simply funny. Funny goes viral.

Touch them with tenderness, and you will give them love. Touch them with love, and you will give them the world. Touch their todays, and you will touch their tomorrows.

JOHNSON & JOHNSON

On Book Marketing Bestsellers I shared book marketing tips that I had learned while watching TV commercials (http://www.bookmarket.com/tvtips.htm). In the blog post, I share a great quote from a TV commercial, and then I comment on how that insight applies to marketing books.

The freshest ideas are right under your nose. (Bounce fabric softener) — Most of your best book ideas and marketing ideas can be found right under your nose. Look around.

Relationships can be a gamble. (Clairol Loving Care) — When entering a relationship with a new distributor or special market, be sure to check them out. Be cautious.

Take time to enjoy the magic. (Disney) — But take time to enjoy everything else as well. Otherwise, what's all the fuss about?

It's amazing what happens when you change everything. (Dodge Intrepid) — If nothing's working, change everything. See what happens.

We're all looking for stories with a happy ending. (Ford) — People like to read about people. They like stories. Make sure all your nonfiction books contain lots of examples and stories. They make the book more interesting. Also write your press releases so they also tell a story.

Touch them with tenderness, and you will give them love. Touch them with love, and you will give them the world. Touch their todays, and you will touch their tomorrows. (Johnson & Johnson) — To build word of mouth for your book, touch people's hearts, or minds, or inner souls.

Rules to live by: Make waves. Blow your own horn. Have your cake and eat it too. (Pontiac Sunfire) — Don't expect someone else to blow your horn. You'll have to take charge yourself.

When you find the destiny to which you were born, all you need to bring with you is your honor, your courage, and your commitment. (U.S. Navy) — The best publishers hold true to their vision.

One author had a great idea: Why not tie into the media and consumer interest in the latest Harry Potter book, which sold millions of copies, and movie. What did he do to piggy-back on this publicity and interest? Very simple. He created a blog about the book's marketing.

Gosh, I wish I had thought to do that. He picked up hundreds of links to his website as a result of his simple (and time-limited) blog hosted on BlogSpot.com.

Not only does he get all these links, but he doesn't have to maintain this blog for very long to get all the value that he has already gotten in less than ten days.

Just think: What upcoming event that will get a lot of interest can you blog about? The new TV season? The hot new TV drama or comedy? The latest reality TV show?

The NFL football season. The NHL getting back into play. The breakup of the big AFL-CIO union as unions go off on their own (this is big news right now in the labor and business markets).

Potter was really big. What's the next big thing? Think about it. Then blog about it. It's so simple to do. When you blog, always include a press release via the Internet as part of the launch of your new blog.

80. Share a joke.

Jokes go viral. Even better if the joke ties into your topic or novel.

In a post on my old book promotion blog, I wrote about using Jokes for Word of Mouse Propagation: https://openhorizons.blogspot.com/2005/05/jokes-for-word-of-mouse-propagation.html. Here's part of a long joke:

One of the best ways to get your message passed on is to include a joke. While your entire message may not get passed on, the joke will be. For example, here's a joke I just received from Ken Darby, who sends out an ezine, which always includes a joke, a saying, and an article that are all available for reprint at any time (with credit at that time).

You may not know that many non-living things have a gender. For example:

Ziploc Bags – They are Male, because they hold everything in, but you can see right through them.

Copiers – They are Female, because once turned off, it takes a while to warm them up again. It's an effective reproductive device if the right buttons are pushed, but can wreak havoc if the wrong buttons are pushed.

Tire – Male, because it goes bald and it's often over-inflated.

Hot Air Balloon – Male, because, to get it to go anywhere, you have to light a fire under it and, of course, there's the hot air component.

Subway – Male, because it uses the same old lines to pick people up.

Hammer – Male, because it hasn't changed much over the last 5,000 years, but it's handy to have around.

People love humor on social networks, so share humor when you can, both on your website and in your social networks.

A positive attitude may not solve all your problems, but it will annoy enough people to make it worth the effort. — Herm Albright

Or this pin:

Or these tweets:

It's called reading. It's how people install new software into their brains. #reading #books

Halloween is just an excuse for men to dress slutty. #Humor

I doubt tequila is the answer but it's worth a shot.

No matter how bad ass you are, you'll never top a raccoon riding an alligator!

When I see rich, snooty looking people at the grocery store: Excuse me, do you work here?

If you don't teach your parrot to say, "Help, they've turned me into a parrot," you're wasting everyone's time.

And I want to share this funny Facebook post from by one of my in-laws celebrating their 55th wedding anniversary:

Celebrating our 55th!

After being married for 55 years this month, I took a careful look at my wife one day and said, "Fifty-five years ago we had a cheap house, a junk car, slept on a sofa-bed, and watched a 10-inch black-and-white TV. But hey I got to sleep every night with a hot 23-year-old girl.

Now ... I have a $750,000 home, a $45,000 car, a nice big bed, and a large screen TV, but I'm sleeping with a 77-year-old woman. So I said to my wife, "It seems to me that you're not holding up your side of things."

My wife is a very reasonable woman. She told me to go out and find a hot 23-year-old girl and she would make sure that I would once again be living in a cheap house, driving a junk car, sleeping on a sofa bed, and watching a 10-inch black-and-white TV.

81. Create a bibliography for your genre or topic.

Feature the best books you recommend. When you create a topic-focused bibliography of recommended books, you establish your expertise and credibility.

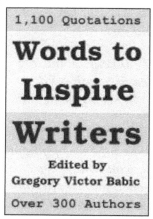

On my BookMarket.com website, I feature a bibliography of books on book publishing, book marketing, publicity, general marketing, direct marketing, and related topics: http://bookmarket.com/1001bib.htm. The bibliography featured over 200 titles. Note: I don't maintain that list anymore and will likely delete it soon.

Here's a wonderful bibliography of books about children and gardening curated by the Floral School: http://www.floralschool.com/pdfs/BibliographyChildren&Flowers-YoungerKids.pdf.

Your list of recommended books should included at least ten books, but can include as many as 200 books. Be sure to include the books of your friends (as well as your own) in your annotated bibliography.

82. Create a glossary for your genre or topic.

Create a dictionary or glossary for your topic or a key related topic. For instance, define some of the key terms for romance novels, for science fiction, for rabbit hunting, for crocheting, for what you write about.

For Book Marketing Bestsellers, I created a Social Networking Glossary: Social Media Words You Should Know: https://bookmarketingbestsellers.com/social-networking-glossary-social-media-words-you-should-know. It included 82 definitions, like these:

Avatar — The main image featured in the member profile of any social network.

Aggregator — *A tool or app that gathers content from various sources and then displays them to an end user. It can aggregate blog posts, status updates (tweets, pins, etc.), or other content.*

Dashboard — *The interface that allows users to monitor their social network activity as well as take actions like sharing content.*

Engagement — *Describes whether or not users get involved with a brand's content on social networks. Engagement can be measured by user actions such as shares, comments, likes, retweets, etc.*

GIFs — *Animated images created in a compressed file format originally developed by CompuServe to share simple icons and images with a palette of no more than 256 colors. Animated GIFs are especially hot on Tumblr blogs.*

Hashtag — *an interactive feature that allows social network users to relate a status update to a broader topic.*

Influencer — *Anyone (blogger, social network user, etc.) who is active in social communities and often able to sway the opinions of others. Brands consider these influencers as their most valuable followers and fans.*

Infographic — *One of the best pieces of content to share any social network, especially Pinterest and Google+ where they feature the entire graphic. Infographics tend to include a detailed visual picture of some content.*

Like — *On Facebook and some other social networks, users can show their approval of a status update with a like. Also, to receive status updates from business pages on Facebook, the user must like the page.*

83. Share a fact.

Give your readers some tidbit they likely don't know about your topic.

This can be a short blog post, something like this: Did you know that 1200 years ago there were probably 12 million kiwis in New Zealand. Today there are only 70,000.

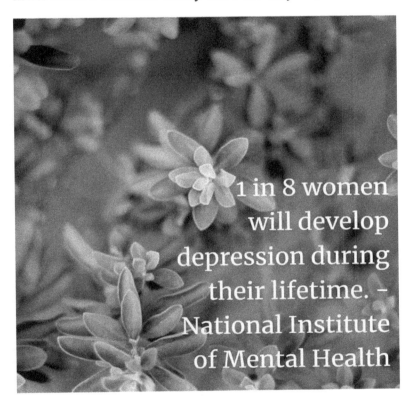

On my Celebrity Weight-Loss Tips website, I recently shared this statistic: *1 in 8 women will develop depression during their lifetime. — National Institute of Mental Health* at http://celebrityweightlosstips.com/women-and-depression.

84. Promote your news.

Let your readers know about your new books, new products, new updates, new services, new podcasts, new videos, etc.

John Kremer
November 23 at 12:10 AM

This is the first episode in the God Bless You Miracle podcasts. I'll be sharing more during the coming days on how to pray to get results — using the God Bless You Miracle program.

http://www.MyIncredibleWebsite.com/God-Bless-You-Miracle

I posted on Facebook to announce my new God Bless You Miracle podcasts (in a new God Bless You Miracle group): https://www.facebook.com/groups/265132610857801.

Of course, you can also send out news releases that will appear on multiple websites besides your own.

Here are three resources that could help you send out lots of news releases:

News Release Critiques

That Help You Sell More Books, Products, Services, or Ideas

News Release Critiques That Help You Sell More Books, Products, Services, or Ideas: https://bookmarketingbestsellers.com/news-release-critiques-that-help-you-sell-more-books-products-services-or-ideas.

Book Publicists, PR Services, and Book Publicity Experts: https://bookmarketingbestsellers.com/book-publicists-and-book-publicity-services-a-to-m.

Free Press Release Distribution Services: https://bookmarketingbestsellers.com/online-and-free-news-release-distribution-services.

85. Blog about new web pages.

When you add new resources or web pages to your website, let your readers know. If you create new websites related to your original website, announce those as well.

For many issues of my Book Marketing Tip of the Week email newsletter, I also posted them on my Book Marketing Bestsellers website. These issues often linked to new web pages (blog posts, videos, resource listings, etc.).

Here are the listings of recent posts from one such issue:

How to Sell Without Selling Your Soul - https://bookmarketingbestsellers.com/how-to-sell-without-selling-your-soul

John Kremer: On the Air with That Literary Lady -
https://bookmarketingbestsellers.com/john-kremer-on-the-air-with-that-literary-lady

Book Marketing Tips on Facebook -
https://bookmarketingbestsellers.com/john-kremers-book-marketing-tips-on-facebook

Kurt Vonnegut: 16 Rules For Writing Fiction –
https://bookmarketingbestsellers.com/kurt-vonnegut-16-rules-for-writing-fiction

Leo Babauta: 14 Observations on Writing –
https://bookmarketingbestsellers.com/leo-babauta-14-observations-on-writing

Jay Abraham: How to Use Bonuses to Sell More Products -
https://bookmarketingbestsellers.com/jay-abraham-how-to-use-bonuses-to-sell-more-products

The Secret to Selling More Books -
https://bookmarketingbestsellers.com/rock-your-soul-marketing-the-secret-to-selling-more-books

> *Here is the secret to selling more books: Love what you do. When marketing your books, do only the things that really inspire you, that move you, that excite you. Then you'll do a great job of marketing.*
>
> *Be true to yourself. Do the promotions that match your heart, your mind, your service. Ignore the rest (or pay someone else to do those things).*

32 Great Reasons to Read a Good Book -
https://bookmarketingbestsellers.com/32-great-reasons-to-read-a-good-book

86. Congratulate someone.

Give them a thumbs up when they publish a new book, launch a new product, do some great service for humanity, have a new baby, get married. You don't have to tie it into your book or topic.

Here's a **tweet** that Melinda Emerson (@SmallBizLady) shared recently to give a thumb's up to me:

@abeasl123 You need @JohnKremer He's the man when it comes to book marketing ideas.

Here's a congratulatory **tweet** for @PhilanthropyAus for changing their governance structure:

And here's a **Facebook** comment from Charles Betterton praising me:

Words of wisdom from John Kremer, THE book marketing expert who has helped sell over a billion books already and is working on the next billion, perhaps including YOURS!

And here's another **Facebook** comment where Charles Betterton praised Brian Tracy:

I do appreciate and recommend the programs from Brian Tracy: *https://www.briantracy.com/catalog/how-to-write-a-book-and-become-a-published-author*

And here another **Facebook** comment from Rosalie Cross, again praising my book and work:

Dear Mr. Kremer, this Thanksgiving I am thankful for you! Your book "1001 Ways to Market Your Book" is THE best book I've ever read on the subject of writing and marketing. Thank you for the many hours you put in to writing and publishing it. - Rosalie Cross

Retweets are also a way to congratulate someone for what they produce.

87. Thank someone publicly.

When someone does something especially nice for you, thank them in public via your blog or social media.

Rekaya Gibson wrote a comment on my Book Marketing Bestsellers blog thanking me for the post I had written:

Great ideas. I am in the process of writing two cookbooks. Thank you for sharing.

John Kremer
November 29 at 2:25 AM · 🌐 ▾   •••

I recently visited a website where they featured 5 reasons why visitors should leave a comment on their website. I liked those reasons and have added a few more reasons why you should comment on other people's blogs. - http://bookmarketingbestsellers.com/10-reasons-to-leave-a-.../

13 Reasons to Leave a Comment on a Blog Post You Love

1. **Most blogs link your name to your website or allow you to include your website link in your comment. This might improve your site ranking on search engines.**

2. **Other readers might click through on your link and visit your website.**

3. **Contribute to the conversation. Did this blog post help you? Do you have something to add?**

When I posted the above image on Facebook, I had made a typo: 13 Reasons to Leave a Comment on a Blog Post **Your** Love.

Lisa Newman caught the typo and let me know right away. So I thanked her publicly on Facebook"

On Twitter, Pinterest, and other social networks, you can join in on the hashtags for #ThankfulThursdays and #ThankYouNoteFriday. A great time to say thank you to people who deserve it.

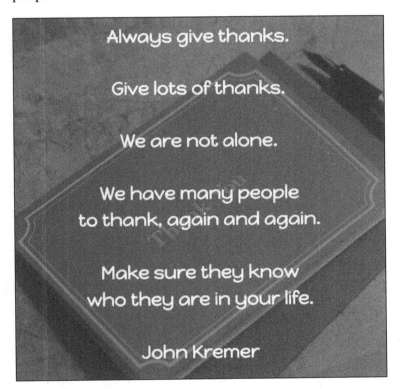

Always give thanks. Give lots of thanks.

We are not alone. We have many people to thank, again and again.

Make sure they know who they are in your life.

And here's an incredible Facebook share from Tony Rubleski, author of *Mind Capture* when commenting on one of my Facebook posts: https://facebook.com/trubleski/posts/10156919101614466.

I commented on his share: *Thanks, Tony, for sharing. Much appreciated.*

And he replied: *You are welcome John! Your work has blessed millions. Grateful you are on this planet at this marker in time.*

88. Make a prediction.

Here's something I tweeted several years ago that has come true: *You heard it here first: The economy has begun to turn the corner. People are beginning to trust themselves again. Good times coming again.*

In January 2016 I described my Holiday Lights Theory of Economics in a blog post. I also made a prediction: https://bookmarketingbestsellers.com/the-holiday-lights-theory-of-economics.

My theory: When people are more optimistic, they take the time to do more holiday decorating. They showcase their optimism via lights on the outsides of their homes.

__The conclusion:__ There are more holiday lights this year. Look for an uptick in the economy during the next year.

__My prediction:__ You will sell more books in 2016. People always read more books when they are happy, hopeful, and prosperous.

And my prediction proved true. Authors and self-publishers did sell more books in 2016, 2017, and 2018. And probably will in 2019 as well.

89. Raise money for a charity.

Offer to donate to a specific charity for every book sold during a specific week or month. Promote this via your blog, tweets, Facebook posts, etc.

I've seen many authors include a charity component to their book launches. On my BookMarket.com website, I share my favorite charitable causes that I donate to regularly: http://www.bookmarket.com/charitablecauses.htm.

10% of all proceeds from sales on this website are donated to the following groups. That means 10% of what you actually pay (excluding postage), not what we net or profit. We like to keep it clean and simple.

When people promise to give 10% or some other percentage of their profits, that means nothing. So many companies, books, etc. don't generate a profit, so 10% of nothing becomes nothing. It's all smoke and mirrors. We actually give 10% of the proceeds from sales via this website's shopping cart to the following causes. Now you know.

Nature Conservancy, American Cancer Society, American Red Cross, Sierra Club, World Wildlife Fund, Multiple Sclerosis Association, Special Olympics, National Wildlife Foundation, Doctors Without Borders, Institute of Noetic Sciences, National Museum of the American Indian, National Audubon Society, The Ocean Conservancy, The

Humane Society of the United States, Worldwatch Institute, American Rivers, Habitat for Humanity, Arthritis Foundation, American Association for the Advancement of Science, National Arbor Day Foundation, Easter Seals, American Lung Association, The Archaeological Conservancy, St. Labre Indian School, St. Jude Children's Research Hospital, The Smithsonian, CARE, National Parks Conservation Association, March of Dimes, National Geographic Society, Alzheimer's Association, UNICEF, Environmental Defense, Cystic Fibrosis Foundation, Paralyzed Vets of America, New Mexico Wilderness Alliance, and American Diabetes Association.

Michael Sullivan, author of the *Forgotten Flowers* novel, offered to donate to Bright Focus in his press releases:

I have recently published a novel titled Forgotten Flowers. It follows the tragic efforts of Daniel Kilgore, living with a wife who suffers from dementia, and his attempt to preserve the dignity and faded memories of three residents in an assisted living facility. I am donating the proceeds my novel to Bright Focus, an organization dedicated to research in the areas of macular degeneration, dementia, and Alzheimer's disease.

90. Ask a provocative question.

Ask provocative questions. Encourage people to share their answers in the comments section for that post.

You don't have to ask the question on your website. You can ask it in a social media post. But be sure to summarize the answers in a blog post.

Joel Comm once tweeted this question: *What would you do if you discovered $100,000 hidden away in your basement?* He got 3.5 pages of replies in less than an hour.

Jeff Rivera asked the following question in a Facebook post: *Do you believe extraterrestrials (aliens from outer space) really exist?* He received 27 replies.

In one poll I conducted on my Book Marketing Success Stories Facebook group, I asked: Are zombies dead or alive? I got few answers.

In another poll in that same Facebook group, I asked: What is your main challenge in self-publishing your books?

Here were the results:

John Kremer created a poll.
March 9, 2017

What is your main challenge in self-publishing your books? You can choose more than one answer if you have multiple challenges. Thanks for participating in this self-publishing poll!

☐ I have no fan club or tribe	+6
☑ time to write my books	+5
☐ I don't know how to market books	+4
☐ time to market my books	+3
☐ money to self-publish my books	

👍❤️ 9   8 Comments

And check out this article where I reprint results from a HubSpot research study by Dan Zarrella: *How to Use Facebook Questions to Increase Social Comments* - https://bookmarketingbestsellers.com/how-to-use-facebook-questions-to-increase-social-comments.

91. Solicit help.

Ask your blog subscribers, newsletter readers, Twitter followers, Facebook fans, and social network connections to help you out when you need help—in your publishing plans, your business, your personal life, your speaking, etc.

When Jeff Rivera was fighting gay prejudice in Costa Rica, he asked his Facebook followers and others to write emails to a list of government leaders and thought leaders in Costa Rica. It helped.

When I was working on my biography, I asked readers to give me feedback on the wording. With their help, this is what I came up with:

Book marketing expert John Kremer is the author of *1001 Ways to Market Your Books*, mentor to authors who have sold over a billion books, and founder of the Billion Book Initiative to help the next generation of book authors sell another billion books. Over the past 30 years, he has helped thousands of authors, both major celebrities and those just starting out, to sell more books!

92. Celebrate milestones.

Blog about your company anniversary, the two-year anniversary of the publication of your book, the 700th post on your blog.

Note: My old book promotion blog had 899 posts. So, just a few moments ago, I wrote one more blog post to make it 900 posts (a nice even number) before I put the blog to pasture: https://openhorizons.blogspot.com/2018/12/a-new-milestone-900-blog-posts.html.

When the 7,000th book author joined The Book Marketing Network (http://www.thebookmarketingnetwork.com), I tweeted about it as well as shared the event in my Book

Marketing Tip of the Week newsletter. The network now has 9,795 members. When it hits 10,000 members, I'll do a big promotion!

What milestone or anniversary can you celebrate? Think about it. Then celebrate it publicly on your website or social media. Here are a few other anniversaries you can celebrate:

Current events—Congdon & Weed published *One American Must Die* to commemorate the anniversary of the terrorist hijacking of a TWA jetliner.

College anniversaries—Globe Pequot Press published *The Illustrated Harvard* to celebrate Harvard's 350th anniversary.

Deaths—Grove Press published Warren Beath's *The Death of James Dean* on the anniversary of Dean's death.

Sports—Donald Fine set the publication date of Maury Alien's *Roger Maris: A Man for All Seasons* to coincide with the 25th anniversary of Maris breaking Babe Ruth's homerun record.

State—Putnam's *Make Way for Sam Houston* tied in with the Texas Sesquicentennial celebration.

TV show—The Library of Congress Read More About It book promotion featured a number of books about soap operas on the 30th anniversary broadcast of *As the World Turns*.

Books—Dutton celebrated the 60th anniversary of the publication of A. A. Milne's classic children's book, *Winnie-the-Pooh*, by publishing *The Winnie-the-Pooh Journal*.

93. Announce awards and honors.

If you receive any awards for your book or honors for yourself, blog about them. Link, of course, to the site of the award giver as well.

When Bob Dylan won the Nobel Prize in Literature, I celebrated his win as the first songwriter to win the Nobel: https://bookmarketingbestsellers.com/bob-dylan-nobel-laureate-in-literature.

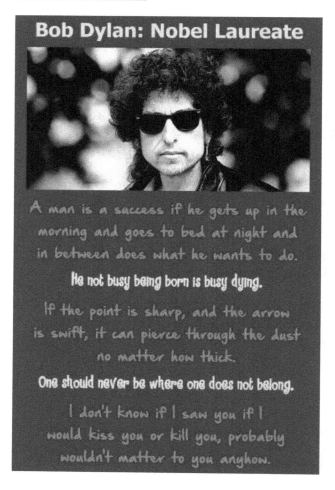

In my Book Marketing Bestsellers blog, I posted the winners of the 2008 Nautilus Book Awards (https://openhorizons.blogspot.com/2008/06/nautilus-book-award-winners-2008.html) – not because I won one of the awards, but simply to celebrate the book authors and publishers who did win.

94. Excerpt your book.

Run a series of excerpts from your book. They can be short paragraphs, tips, entire chapters, a story, whatever you want to share. Or a short ebook featuring 30 pages of your book.

In a post on my Book Marketing Bestsellers website, I shared a story from Nat Bodian's *The Joy of Publishing*: https://bookmarketingbestsellers.com/the-joy-of-publishing-how-to-know-if-a-book-is-good.

You can order this great book by Nat Bodian on Amazon: https://amzn.to/2UedbPe.

95. Ask for feedback.

You can ask for feedback on your blog posts. Ask for feedback on your website design. Ask for feedback on your social media posts. Ask for feedback on your book covers. There are many things you can ask for feedback on.

Here are a few questions you can ask your blog readers, website visitors, or social media followers to encourage them to give your feedback on your current content:

What's your biggest challenge with xxx? (again related to what you shared).

Now it's your turn. What do you think? What one piece of advice would you give a friend to help xxx?

Here's a request I asked my website visitors at the end of a blog post: https://bookmarketingbestsellers.com/the-month-of-thanksgiving-thanks-for-the-little-things.

By the way, thank you for reading this.

If you read this, please leave a comment below. Much appreciated!

96. Share personal stories.

Talk about your family, your health, your relationships, your hobbies, your pets, etc.

I tweeted and posted on Facebook when I had a heart attack scare a while ago. Not only did it personalize me for my followers and fans, but it encouraged me when I received so many good wishes.

Your shared personal story can be funny, serious, moving, passionate, inspirational, educational, informative, even boring.

Two and a half years ago, I wrote a story about an old friend of mine, Willy Mathes, and his invitation to blog at Huffington Post: https://bookmarketingbestsellers.com/a-huffington-post-story-relationships-matter.

An old friend of mine, Willy Mathes, recently had a wonderful bit of writing success.

Willy's been a freelance book editor and writing coach for 17 years. One of his clients, Judy Warren, began blogging for Huffington Post last July. Not long ago, she also started practicing Transcendental Meditation (TM), something Willy had been doing for 43 years. It turns out Arianna Huffington, who invited Judy to blog for Huffington Post during a Women in the Media Who Meditate conference, had also been doing TM for many years.

Since Willy had been wanting to blog about how some principles that help improve writing can also be used to improve one's personal life, he asked Judy to make an e-introduction to Arianna.

Shortly thereafter, Arianna warmly invited Willy to blog for the Huffington Post. On March 16th, they published Willy's post, "Trust the Voice Within You."

97. Have your dog or cat write a blog post.

Chances are, of course, that you'll have to write the post, but do it in the voice of your pet.

Here's a tweet of one person on Twitter:

> *Thinking of starting a tweeter for my dog. Y'all should follow him. He's funny.*

And here's a dog on Twitter who has since left Twitter (alas!).

> *I like sleeping on top of a pile of clothes!*

> *I love being able to shit wherever I want.*

> *I'm home alone! Locked in a room! Save me!!!*

And here are a few tweets from Grumpy Cat's official Twitter profile: https://twitter.com/RealGrumpyCat.

Make this Christmas the Worst one yet. Grumpy Cat's #WorstChristmasEver Available on Streaming and DVD at: iTunes, Amazon, Target, and WalMart

Enough with the cheer already. ALL NEW Grumpy Cat Holiday Wallpapers Available now on @Zedge

Grumpy Cat is on the November cover of @readersdigest! Get your copy today! Or don't.

Happy Holidays? How about... NO. But - I am getting ready for the @GrinchMovie, in theaters this Friday. #TheGrinch has the right idea. #ad

TODAY!!! Meet Grumpy Cat at The Mall of America for the terrible #CatScratchParty 12-3pm in the Rotunda (wristbands are limited - come early) #Minnesota #Minneapolis #StPaul

Worst #Halloween Ever

#NationalDogDay again?

98. Invite family members to blog.

Ask your wife, husband, child, mother, father, or favorite aunt to write a guest blog post. The post can be about you, your book, your website, or whatever they want to write about.

Key tip: A young child writing about your book can be an incredible sales message. Children are cute. We fall for them very easily. If you don't have a child of your own, ask your niece, your neighbor's kid, a school volunteer, or other young person recommended by a teacher, a pastor, or a friend.

At Book Expo America, I've watched children outsell their parents multiple times. Children are not afraid to approach strangers. They are not afraid to make bold statements. And they are rarely afraid to make the sale.

On my catch-all website, My Incredible Website, my wife shares her short, short stories. She writes the stories and I then create graphics to go along with her stories. These are some of the most popular posts on my website.

Here's one of my wife's short short stories: http://www.myincrediblewebsite.com/believe.

One night the turtle said to his friend the frog: "Would you like to fly with me through the stars tonight to meet the moon?"

The frog, who thought the turtle a silly kidder, replied, "Turtle, I don't believe anyone can fly, much less a fellow who carries a shell such as yours."

"Well, come with me tonight and see for yourself," replied the turtle.

Believe

One night the turtle said to his friend the frog: "Would you like to fly with me through the stars tonight to meet the moon?"

The frog, who thought the turtle a silly kidder, replied, "Turtle, I don't believe anyone can fly, much less a fellow who carries a shell such as yours."

"Well, come with me tonight and see for yourself," replied the turtle.

The frog, thinking to catch his friend in a tall tale, said that he would go.

That night, the frog crawled up on the turtle's back and, sure enough, they flew up through the stars to meet the moon.

And do you know the most wondrous part of the whole adventure? Friend frog never again questioned another friend's truth.

Short story by Gail Berry

Source: http://www.myincrediblewebsite.com/believe

The frog, thinking to catch his friend in a tall tale, said that he would go.

That night, the frog crawled up on the turtle's back and, sure enough, they flew up through the stars to meet the moon.

And do you know the most wondrous part of the whole adventure? Friend frog never again questioned another friend's truth.

You can find more of my wife's stories here: http://www.myincrediblewebsite.com/short-stories.

My wife is also the author of two children's books. See her book covers below:

Little Fox and the Golden Hawk

Crazy Horse

Gail Berry

99. Invite your friend to write a guest blog post.

You can invite anyone you want to write for your blog or website: a friend, a neighbor, a business associate, your favorite librarian, your favorite bookseller, the carry out boy at your local grocer, your favorite postal worker, or even a stranger on the street.

Again, they can write about you, your book, your website, or whatever they want to write about. Your choice.

Here's a guest post written by an author friend of mine: https://bookmarketingbestsellers.com/sell-more-books-by-giving-away-your-books. It showcases a key point I often make when talking to authors: Sell more books by giving away books.

I started by releasing Book One of my series, Related by Blood, for free on Amazon. I've also given away Book Two to a select group of readers as well. So far, I've given away more than 1,300 copies in the Related by Blood series, which have resulted in praise from readers such as:

> *"It grabs you by the throat and doesn't let you go until the last page. A real scorching page turner."*

> *"It had me hooked from the start. After finishing it, I wanted more."*

> *"Left me dangling, gasping for breath."*

I'll continue to give away as many free copies of Related by Blood Book One as possible, knowing that readers will get hooked and buy the rest of the series.

100. Create a scavenger hunt.

Get readers excited by asking them to go on a scavenger hunt with you. Have them do the scavenger hunt on your blog, on your website, in your book, or via your social media posts.

Ask your readers to find a specific blog post where you wrote about a specific topic.

Or have them find three specific passages in your book.

Or find three webpages on your website.

This scavenger hunt can be a great tool to encourage people to explore your book, blog, or website in greater depth.

A few minutes ago, I decided to run a scavenger hunt on my personal Facebook profile (where I have the most followers on Facebook).

Scavenger hunt! *In a recent blog post on my website at https://www.bookmarketingbestsellers.com, I wrote about*

*how you can change the world. Find that post and let me
know by private Facebook message where you found it (the
website URL will do).*

*All those who find the post will get a special gift from me,
one I'm sure you will like.*

So start scavenger hunting and let me know what you find!

You, too, can qualify for this scavenger hunt. Let me know
if you find the article and you, too, can win the prize!

101. Solicit money.

If you need to raise funds for the reprinting of your book or to produce a book trailer, create a Kickstarter.com project or a GoFundMe page and promote it through your blog, your podcast, and your social media.

Better yet, have your child create the project and let them write about it on your blog. As I noted a few pages ago, children can be very effective promoters of their parent's work.

Note: Kickstarter is primarily for raising money to create a new product, fund an art project or book or movie, etc. Go Fund Me, on the other hand, is all about raising money for sick people, sick animals, and sick politicians ☺.

Ariana Pluchinsky used Kickstarter to raise funds for her LGBT fantasy novel. *Leah's life flips around in this LGBT fantasy when she becomes the getaway driver for the city's most infamous gang, the Goldfinch.*

She tweeted about her campaign (see the next page). At the time, she was just a few hundred dollars from reaching her $6,000 goal to fund the creation and printing of volume one in her graphic novel series.

Pat the Builder tweeted about his Kickstarter campaign to make a documentary:

I have just launched my Kickstarter campaign in order to make a documentary about life in the world's northernmost town, Longyearbyen!! Please spread the word and help in anyway you can!

Jeff Speziale tweeted about his Kickstarter campaign for *The Monster Book of Monsters* horror anthology.

Tis the season!
https://www.kickstarter.com/projects/mbom/the-monster-
book-of-monsters-film-project ... #horror #creepypasta
#Anthology #Kickstarter

For additional fund-raising platforms, see my blog post at
https://bookmarketingbestsellers.com/crowdfunding-
websites.

And for tips on doing a crowdfunding campaign, see https://bookmarketingbestsellers.com/11-keys-to-crowdfunding-success.

11 Keys to Crowdfunding Success

Pick the right platform for your project.

Create a kick-ass video.

Offer rewards for different levels of donations.

Set a large enough goal.

Scale to the size of your social network.

Set a 30-day timeline (not 60 days).

Pitch your friends and fans.

Build your network early.

Hit it big from Day One.

Never turn off.

Fail fast.

More details here:
BookMarketingBestsellers.com/crowdfunding-websites

102. Recruit joint venture partners.

When you are working on a product launch, an Amazon Bestseller Campaign, or a blog tour, solicit partners via your blog and social networks. Write about what you propose to do and ask your readers if they want to help. You can solicit JV partners for any promotion campaign.

Book Marketing Makeover Months Redux

In December 2011 and January 2012, I featured guest posts from book authors, publicists, service providers, and others. Some of that book marketing content is still relevant today (seven years later), so I'm sharing the most relevant guest articles here on this website or linked to the original article on my old book promotion blog.

Social Media: Pros and Cons – Should You Join the Fray? – Brian Feinblum:
https://openhorizons.blogspot.com/2011/12/social-media-pros-and-cons-should-you.html

Top 15 Reasons to Do a Virtual Book Tour – Dana Lynn Smith:
https://openhorizons.blogspot.com/2011/12/book-marketing-makeover-top-15-reasons.html

Dead Body Cookies Create Killer Sales for Mystery Novel – Cindy Sample:
https://bookmarketingbestsellers.com/dead-body-cookies-create-killer-sales-for-mystery-novel

Writing Contest Promotes Las Vegas Novel – Avery Cardoza:
https://bookmarketingbestsellers.com/writing-contest-promotes-las-vegas-novel

Writing Effective Emails That Get Attention – Jill Konrath:
https://bookmarketingbestsellers.com/writing-effective-emails-that-get-attention

Query Letters That Work: Grab Them with the First Sentence – Jeff Rivera:
https://bookmarketingbestsellers.com/query-letters-that-work-grab-them-with-the-first-sentence

---

On my blog at The Book Marketing Network, I ask members to send me a guest blog post to celebrate Book Marketing Makeover Months during December 2011 and January 2012. You can check out the blog post here: http://thebookmarketingnetwork.com/profiles/blogs/guest-blog-post-during-book-marketing-makeover-months-in-december.

During the months of December and January, I'm featuring interviews with other book authors and book marketing stars on their key tips for marketing their books successfully. Also success stories, questions, and more.

Please participate. It won't cost you a dime—and you'll get incredible link love.

You could be part of this special event. Simply email me with your answers to two to three or all of the following questions:

> *How large is your platform or network? Did you use your platform or network in marketing your book? If so, how?*

> *Are you involved in any social networks? Have you used them in marketing your book? Again, if so, how?*

> *Have you created and posted any online videos? Did any of them go viral? How many people viewed them?*

> *What publicity produced the best results in terms of book sales? Magazines, newspapers, radio, TV? Which TV shows or magazines created the most impact?*

> *Did you speak to promote your book? If so, what audiences or venues produced the best sales?*

> *What Internet marketing technique produced the best sales results for your book? Did you do anything interesting to boost the effectiveness of the technique?*

> *What book marketing technique produced the best sales results for your book? Give some details or tell a story on how you carried out your marketing campaign.*

Instead of answering all these questions, if you have a good story to tell—that would be just as good. Even preferable.

After answering the above questions, please also send me your name and website or blog, plus a short sales message.

This information will be featured at the end of your interview.

Your interview and link will be featured on one of my websites. Links from my website are guaranteed to increase the traffic to your website as well as improve your Alexa ranking and Google love.

You can check out many of the resulting guest posts and articles here: https://bookmarketingbestsellers.com/book-marketing-makeover-months-redux.

Here are the first six articles:

Social Media: Pros and Cons – Should You Join the Fray? – https://openhorizons.blogspot.com/2011/12/social-media-pros-and-cons-should-you.html

Top 15 Reasons to Do a Virtual Book Tour – https://openhorizons.blogspot.com/2011/12/book-marketing-makeover-top-15-reasons.html

Dead Body Cookies Create Killer Sales for Mystery Novel – https://bookmarketingbestsellers.com/dead-body-cookies-create-killer-sales-for-mystery-novel

Writing Contest Promotes Las Vegas Novel – https://bookmarketingbestsellers.com/writing-contest-promotes-las-vegas-novel

Writing Effective Emails That Get Attention – https://bookmarketingbestsellers.com/writing-effective-emails-that-get-attention

Query Letters That Work: Grab Them with the First Sentence – https://bookmarketingbestsellers.com/query-letters-that-work-grab-them-with-the-first-sentence

103. Create a holiday.

Anyone can create a new holiday, commemorative week or month, special day of recognition, or other sort of annual celebration. The Celebrate Today Special Events Data Files feature over 19,000 such special events.

Mother's Day, Father's Day, and Memorial Day were all days created by individuals or organizations. Take Your Daughter to Work Day was created by the National Organization of Women.

I've created a number of holidays, including Business and Reference Books Month celebrated during January, Use More of Your Mind Day celebrated on January 11 (the birthday of William James), International Book Publishers Day celebrated on January 16 (my birthday), and many more.

What day, week, or month could you create to promote your book, the topic of your book, or a keyword related to your product or service?

In one post on my Book Marketing Bestsellers blog (https://openhorizons.blogspot.com/2005/08/celebrate-pod-and-e-books-this-month.html), I wrote the following:

I think it's appropriate to celebrate POD (print-on-demand) and ebooks during August, especially since it's National Publish Your eBook Month!

That month was created by another book author, yet I promoted it. So you don't have to create your own holiday to celebrate a special event on your blog, website, or social media. You can celebrate a holiday someone else created as well.

For the 2018 Nanowrimo (National Novel Writing Month), I created several special offers for book authors. Among them were the following:

Custom QuoteGraphics for Your Blog Posts and Social Media *— Get the special price now during December on custom quotegraphics for your book or product.*

Special Discount on Book Title Critique *— Get a book title that will really help you sell more books. Normally $150. This month, only $100.*

Special Discount on News Release Critique *— John will help you develop a news release that gets the attention of the media and traffic from consumers.*

Great Books Are Found Everywhere Video *— Get a custom book promotion video and social graphics for a pittance! You have to check out this special Great Books video for your book! Two great examples!*

Book Marketing Consultation with John Kremer *— Half price for an hour of consultation with John Kremer during December. Ask your most important and crucial book marketing, self-publishing, and book publishing questions.*

Tip-O-Graphics Create Powerful Traffic to Your Book Sites *— Get an exclusive tip-o-graphic created for your book, novel, product, service, idea, or cause. Tip-o-graphics drive traffic to your website, social media, Amazon book page, or anywhere else you want more traffic.*

You can order the Celebrate Today Special Events Data Files by clicking here: https://BookMarket.Checkout-Secured.com/shop/cgi/shop/cart/add?shopID=12&prodID=16442&qty=1.

As for the special offers for Nanowrimo, check out my BookMarketingBestsellers.com website at the beginning of November. I do special offers every year, not only for novelists, but for other book authors and internet marketers as well.

104. Ask for contributions to a new book.

Ask people for stories you could add to a book you are writing. But be sure to offer them credit for their stories with a link to their website.

I'm always looking for new stories on how authors have marketed their books. That's one reason I created the Book Marketing Success Stories group on Facebook: https://www.facebook.com/groups/BookMarketingSuccess Stories. Authors share some wonderful success stories in that group.

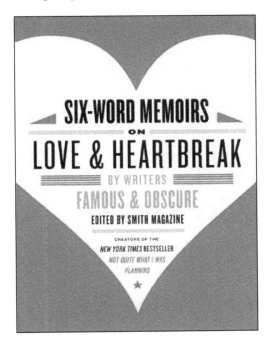

Here are some sample 6-word memoirs from the book *Six-Word Memoirs on Love & Heartbreak*. I bet the authors solicited many of these memoirs via their blog or social networks.

Married by Elvis, divorced by Friday.

It's like my heart has sciatica.

It's worth it, despite your mother.

She defines happiness, I defy gravity.

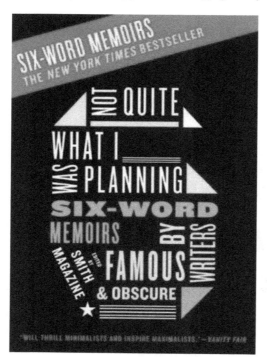

And more stories they've shared in *Not Quite What I Was Planning*, a *New York Times* bestseller.

Savior complex makes for many disappointments.

I like big butts, can't lie.

Cursed with cancer. Blessed with friends.

I still make coffee for two.

Before writing the end chase scene for *Dying for a Deal*, Cindy Sample, author of the Laurel McKay mystery series, asked her website visitors and social media followers to help her choose their favorite movie or television chase scene: https://cindysamplebooks.com/2017/06/help-choose-chase-scene.

I was determined to write a truly unique chase in Dying for a Date, the first book in my Laurel McKay Mysteries. Unless some other author has written a scene consisting of dueling backhoes, I think I succeeded. Slowest chase scene ever, but it will make you giggle....

Dying for a Dance upped the suspense when I created a snowmobile chase on the shores of Lake Tahoe. Then things really heated up in Dying for a Daiquiri when the action moved to balmy Hawaii, and Laurel ends up being chased by a crazed killer on a zip line. Laurel declared it so harrowing her screams could be heard 2,500 miles away in Sacramento....

But I do need your help crafting my latest chase scene in Dying for a Deal. Much of the action takes place in the Lake Tahoe area, but this time during the summer. There are so many options to choose from. Paddle-boards, jet skis, year-round gondolas or an old-fashioned sternwheeler. Help me choose or come up with an original idea of your own.

105. Share a mistake.

Admit it when you make a mistake. It makes you human. Humans are more fun to read.

In a comment on a guest blog post on my old blog (https://openhorizons.blogspot.com/2009/05/7-costly-mistakes-to-avoid-when.html), I admitted to allowing a typo to get into the post. My fault. And I said so.

That was my mistake, not the author's mistake. My fault for being too much in a hurry to post the entry.

Of course, that error has been corrected in the blog post, so you won't find that error. But perhaps you will find another one. Let me know.

Conclusion

People care about novelists and book authors. You don't have to be perfect. You don't have to be professorial. You don't have to be journalistic. Tell the truth. Keep it simple. Cut a vein and let it bleed on the screen.

The above list can also be used by internet marketers, bloggers, Shopify store owners, podcasters, membership site owners, email newsletter editors, and more.

Fiction writers often ask what they should blog about. Or what they should write articles about. Or what they should do for press releases. But those same concerns are common to most newbies on the Internet or in social media.

The above ideas, obviously, can be used for more than blogging. You can use these ideas to help you with the following writing and marketing activities:

Write articles for syndication.

Write press releases.

Create new products and services.

Write newsletter articles.

Create videos.

Write posts for your Facebook page, profile, or group.

Tweet on Twitter.

Pin on Pinterest.

Post on LinkedIn.

Post on Instagram.

Create new website pages.

Write guest posts.

Post on any social media.

Share on your GoodReads page.

Create audios.

Compile ideas for new books.

Come up with ideas for new speeches.

Create new seminars and webinars.

Those are just a few of the ways you can use the 105 content ideas presented in this book.

This book has been about personal blogging for authors, experts, and plain old people.

The next book in the series will be about content marketing in a really serious way. In that book, we will cover incredible ways to use content marketing to build targeted traffic, get more search engine visibility, and make more sales. This coming book will be for serious professionals ready and willing to create traffic-getting content.

John Kremer on Social Networks

You can follow me on any of these social networks. I'd be glad if you did, and I would follow you back.

You should follow lots of people on social networks. That's how you begin to create real relationships with key influencers and fellow authors. Those relationships are the golden key for your selling more books.

Facebook: John Kremer and Book Marketing

Personal Profile: https://www.facebook.com/johnkremer

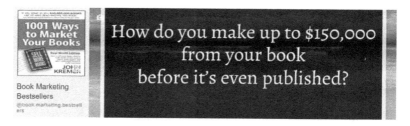

Keyword Page:
https://www.facebook.com/book.marketing.bestsellers

Book Marketing Success Stories group:
https://www.facebook.com/groups/BookMarketingSuccess Stories

John Kremer on Twitter

John Kremer profile: https://www.twitter.com/johnkremer

Book Marketing Tips: https://twitter.com/bookmarkettips

John Kremer on LinkedIn

John Kremer: https://www.linkedin.com/in/johnkremer

====

John Kremer on Pinterest

John Kremer: https://www.pinterest.com/johnkremer

====

John Kremer on YouTube

https://www.youtube.com/user/JohnKremer

John Kremer
62 subscribers

HOME   VIDEOS   PLAYLISTS   CHANNELS   DISCUSSIO

Book Marketing Tips from John Kremer

Book Marketing Tips Playlist
John Kremer · Updated 6 days ago

5 Keys to Self Publishing Success · 7:37
Make Money Before You Publish Your Book · 0:43

VIEW FULL PLAYLIST (11 VIDEOS)

About the Author

Book marketing expert John Kremer is the author of *1001 Ways to Market Your Books*, mentor to authors who have sold over a billion books, and founder of the Billion Book Initiative to help the next generation of book authors sell another billion books.

Over the past 34 years, he has helped thousands of authors, both major celebrities and those just starting out, to sell more books! Lots more books!